I0046155

The 21 Best Cashflow Niches™
Creating Wealth In The Best Alternative Cashflow Investments

By
M.C. Laubscher

The 21 Best Cashflow Niches™

Copyright © 2021 by Cashflow Ninja Publishing®

Authored by M.C. Laubscher

Edited by Elizabeth Hagenlocher

Published by Cashflow Ninja Publishing®

All rights reserved. Printed in the United States of America. No part of this publication may be reproduced, stored in a retrieval system or transmitted in any form or by any means, electronic, mechanical, photocopying, recording or otherwise without the written permission of the author and publisher: Cashflow Ninja Publishing®.

ISBN: (Paperback)   978-1-7378834-1-8

ISBN: (Digital)   978-1-7378834-0-1

First Print Edition

October 2021

Cashflow Ninja LLC

2110 S Eagle Road #403

Newtown, PA 18940

www.cashflowninja.com

Disclaimer:

The information presented in this book is for informational purposes only. It does not constitute professional financial, tax, legal, or investment advice. Neither the publisher nor the author guarantees or promises the results that you may obtain from it.

The author and the publisher do not provide legal, tax or any other advice.

Every situation is unique, and this book discusses generalities that may not be applicable to your unique situation. You should seek your own advice from professional advisors, including lawyers, financial advisors, and accountants, regarding the legal, tax and financial implications of any investment you contemplate. This book is not a substitute for professional advice that is customized to your unique situation.

At press time, the author and publisher, have made reasonable efforts to ensure that the information presented in this book was correct. However, there are no representations that the information will continue to be accurate. The author and publisher hereby disclaim any and all liability to any other party for any loss, damage, or cost arising from or related to the accuracy or completeness in this book, regardless of the cause.

Neither the author and publisher should be held liable or responsible to any person or entity if any information, commentary, analysis, opinions, advice and or recommendations contained in this book, directly or indirectly result in any incidental, indirect, or consequential damages and losses.

Disclaimer

The information present in this book is for informational purposes only. It does not constitute professional, financial, or legal investment advice. Neither the author nor the author guarantees or promises the results that you may wish to achieve.

The author and the publisher do not provide legal, tax, or any other advice.

Every situation is unique, and the advice offered in this book may not be applicable to your unique situation. You should seek your own advice from professional advisors, including lawyers and accountants, and as suitable regarding the legal, tax, and financial implications of any investment you contemplate taking. As such, it is advisable for professional advice that you consult to your individual circumstances.

At press time, the author made all of the necessary due diligence efforts to ensure that the information presented in this book was correct. However, there are no representations and the information will continually be accurate. The author and publisher hereby disclaim any and all liability to any other party for any damage or loss of this book, the related to the accuracy or completeness in this book, resulting from negligence.

Neither the author nor publisher should be held liable or responsible to any person or entity for any information, error, analysis, opinion, or advice and/or recommendation contained in this book, directly or indirectly results in any damage, financial or commercial, incidental damages, and losses.

This book is dedicated to our amazing global community of Cashflow Ninjas all over the world that live their freedom, and legacy TODAY on their own terms.

Acknowledgements

So many people to thank!

A big thank you to my editor Elizabeth Hagenlocher that is simply a pleasure to work with and helped bring my ideas to life on paper.

I am so grateful for every guest that I get to interview on my show, Cashflow Ninja®.

Thank you for spending time with me and sharing your journey and knowledge with me and my listeners and viewers.

I am so blessed with the incredible friends, business partners, and mentors that continue to challenge me to dream and think bigger every day.

Thank you to my amazing family for their unconditional love and support throughout my life.

The person most responsible for my vision becoming reality is my partner in marriage, business and life, my wife Megan.

My children, Christian and Josephine, gave me the gift of an incredible purpose I could not have dreamed possible.

Book Bonuses:

By purchasing this book, you also receive the following bonuses:

A digital version of the book

An audio version of the book

Curated podcast interviews of Cashflow Ninjas sharing The 21 Best Cashflow Niches™

Bonus video interviews

Please e-mail the team at Cashflow Ninja® at info@cashflowninja.com a copy of your purchase receipt and you will be granted access asap.

Contents

Introduction

Fellow Freedom Seeker,

I have been blessed to create a platform, Cashflow Ninja®, that has allowed me to interview the best minds in the world in business, investing, economics and finance.

I have gained valuable insights from these great minds and learned how to create, protect, and multiply wealth in any economy and in any market.

I have been honored that my podcast, Cashflow Ninja®, has been consistently featured as one of the top business and investing podcasts. The podcast has also been recognized as one of the top 48 podcasts for entrepreneurs by *Entrepreneur Magazine*.

When I started my podcast, I would never have imagined that it would have been downloaded millions of times and listened to in over 180 countries.

Since I started my show, I have received many questions about what I have learned from my guests, but the most frequently asked questions have been:

1) Why do the majority of people struggle financially?

2) What do wealthy people do differently than the majority of people that struggle financially?

3) What have been the best investment niches shared on your show?

4) How do you invest in these niches?

5) How do you get access to the best investment opportunities in these niches?

In this book, I share what I have learned from my guests regarding these questions, focusing on the 21 best cash flow niches shared by my guests on the Cashflow Ninja® podcast.

Before we dive into the best cash flow niches, let's see why most people struggle financially. What do wealthy Cashflow Ninjas do to build and grow their wealth regardless of the economy and markets?

"If you don't understand the problem, the solution does not matter" – R. Nelson Nash

Through my conversations with Cashflow Ninjas, I have understood why most people lose in the game of capital and wealth.

There are many reasons why most people struggle financially. In contrast, a tiny percentage of people and families continue to grow their wealth. I have identified the top five reasons that continue to come up in conversations with the world's leading experts in business, investing, economics and finance.

1) Paradigm, Worldview, Mindset, Beliefs, Belief Systems, Models And Frameworks

I learned from Cashflow Ninjas how powerful our beliefs are. We will never change and improve our lives in areas that we want to improve if we do not change our beliefs and our belief systems.

We do not get to choose when and where we are born, who our parents are, what religion we are birthed into, who our neighbors are and what community, town, city, state and country we grow up in.

We adopt from birth the paradigm, worldview, mindset, beliefs and belief systems, models and frameworks of our parents, family, friends, and community.

Our paradigm is the lens through which we see the world. It determines our worldview and mindset. At the core of our paradigm are our beliefs and belief systems.

Changing our beliefs about money and wealth is one of the hardest things to do. Most of our beliefs are rooted in fear and scarcity. That is why so few people are successful in doing it.

Our beliefs are sacred to us. People would rather defend their beliefs and belief systems than evaluate and reconsider them based on logic, reason, evidence, solid fact patterns, and critical thinking.

It's very hard to reason yourself out of beliefs and belief systems that you did not reason yourself into in the first place. That is why so few people can do that.

The majority of people also adopt models and frameworks to navigate the world from their parents, family, friends, teachers, and professors that are unproven and massively flawed.

Like our beliefs, we instinctively defend and protect models and frameworks even though they are flawed. We defend and protect models even if they did not produce the results we desire for the people from which we adopted them.

Models and frameworks are how we make sense of our world and process and interpret data and information.

Our foundational building blocks are our paradigm, worldview, mindset, and beliefs and beliefs systems, models and frameworks. If these blocks are flawed, it is impossible to make good decisions since we cannot distinguish between good, solid real data and information and flawed, incorrect, skewed and biased data and information.

These fundamental building blocks impact the quality of our thinking and the quality of the questions we ask ourselves. It also determines the quality of our lives.

The data and information we use to make decisions are based on these fundamental building blocks, impacting the quality of our decisions that affect our lives.

You can overcome limiting beliefs and belief systems that hold you back and contribute to your paradigm, change your worldview and mindset of scarcity. Then, embracing a paradigm and worldview of gratitude and abundance with a perspective focused on growth would open up a world to opportunities you could not even dream of.

The wealthiest people on the planet understand the power of their paradigm and worldview, their mindset, beliefs, and belief systems. They make it a priority to focus on continuous improvement and development in this area.

They use proven and established models and frameworks to navigate the world. They are always open to adjusting them when the facts change and new solid fact patterns emerge.

The wealthiest people use the scientific method to develop a working hypothesis for models and frameworks and to include new elements into their models and frameworks.

When the facts change and solid fact patterns emerge contrary to their models and frameworks, they change and adjust their models.

The wealthiest people on the planet are always trying to figure out a better way to do things. They are constantly looking for knowledge and information of which they are unaware.

They are always open to new and better ways to do things that would increase productivity efficiency and potentially multiply their efforts.

Wealthy people value what they invest in and invest heavily in their paradigm, worldview, mindset, and models and frameworks.

They know that they themselves are their greatest asset and invest in themselves by investing in their mindset, skill sets and capabilities, and relationships and networks.

"More gold has been mined from the thoughts of men than has been taken from the earth." – Napoleon Hill, *Think & Grow Rich*

2) The Game Of Capital And Wealth

Most people are not aware that there is a game of capital and wealth.

They do not understand the game's rules, know who the players are and how the best players play the game to win consistently.

The majority of people also do not understand financial capital, what it is, how it works, and how wealth is created and distributed.

They also do not understand that there are many forms of capital, of which financial capital is only one form. Ethan Roland has shared eight forms of capital[1]: social, material, financial, living, intellectual, experiential, spiritual, and cultural.

The wealthiest people on the planet know and understand the game of capital and wealth, know the rules, and know who the players are.

They are lifelong students of the game, and they know that teams play the game. Therefore, they build a wealth team to help them implement and execute strategies in the game to win and to continue to win.

Because the wealthy understand the game, the rules, and how to play like the best players, they have access to opportunities that most of the population does not have access to.

So how do the wealthy play the game?

The wealthy understand how the global banking and financial system operates. They know the difference between money, currency and fiat currency.

They understand the history of money. Every country in the world had had a fiat currency since 1971, when Richard Nixon took the world completely off the gold standard.

---

[1] http://www.appleseedpermaculture.com/8-forms-of-capital/

They know that fiat currencies are not backed by anything right now. Fiat currencies are issued by a decree and fiat of governments and are enforced through countries' legal tender laws.

They know that central banks set the monetary policy of their countries. Central banks determine the price of fiat currencies by managing interest rates and the fiat currency supply of the countries in which they are located.

They know in a debt-based monetary system, governments that determine fiscal policy will continue to spend and rack up more debt.

They understand that the value of fiat currency will be diluted by design. They know how to position themselves to benefit from the result of an increasing fiat currency supply, inflation.

Wealthy people own assets, such as businesses that generate capital for them through the value that these businesses provide to the marketplace through their products and services.

Business owners take on risk as entrepreneurs and create jobs. The tax code then rewards business owners.

Business owners can also collateralize assets of their businesses to access more capital from lending institutions to grow their businesses.

The tax-efficient income and capital they generate from their businesses are then warehoused in institutions that benefit society as a whole, like life insurance companies.

By warehousing their capital in permanent life insurance vehicles with insurance companies, they receive guarantees on their principal and tax-free growth. They receive tax-free dividends, and they can access their capital tax-free to grow their businesses and invest in hard assets. They are also able to transfer capital tax-free to their estate.

Banks allocate most of their Tier 1 capital similarly, as do Fortune 500 corporations with their capital reserves.

After the wealthy generate capital and warehouse and protect it, the capital is then leveraged and deployed into hard assets like real estate and energy projects that again provides maximum value to society. Therefore, they receive favorable tax treatment.

They benefit society by providing affordable housing and investment in energy projects to develop cleaner and more environmentally friendly energy.

Wealthy people generate, warehouse, and invest capital. They can increase their wealth contractually every year and pay very little or almost no tax.

In 2020, there was an expansion in the fiat currency supply (25% of all U.S. dollars were created of ALL dollars ever created in 2020[2]). In times like these, institutions, corporations, and wealthy individuals and families will access the new fiat currency units and position it in assets like businesses and real estate.

This allows them to borrow even more fiat currency at low rates.

They will benefit from asset inflation since the value of the businesses and real estate will increase. They will also benefit from price inflation because they can increase the prices of the products and services of their businesses and increase the rent from their real estate properties.

Business owners and investors can borrow capital at very low rates to grow their businesses and investment portfolio. The growth of their businesses and investments are treated very favorably from a tax standpoint because of the value that it provides.

The middle class has some assets such as their houses and retirement plans, but they do not see increases in their income to keep up with inflation.[3]

---

[2] https://fred.stlouisfed.org/series/M1

[3] https://www.epi.org/publication/charting-wage-stagnation/

If they see income increases, they will also see an increase in the amount of taxes they pay through the graduated tax system.

When the crumbs get to the poor, they get hit by price inflation. Everything they need for survival (housing, food, clothes) becomes more expensive. Their incomes do not increase as the costs of everything they need do.

The poor also do not have access to capital at low rates. They pay loan shark interest rates at payday loan service providers and the highest interest rates in the economy on their credit cards. (20% or more[4])

Richard Cantillon[5] was an economist that saw that newly created "money" is never distributed equally throughout the economy. Instead, institutions, families and individuals closest to centers of influence and power had access first to the newly created "money" before it spread throughout the economy.

We have a classic "Cantillon Effect" present in the global economy today.

The wealthy understand the "Cantillon Effect" and the game of capital and wealth. They increase their wealth regardless of the economy, markets and who the president is.

They position themselves to benefit from debt, taxes, and inflation.

Many millionaires and billionaires were created in 2020, while at the same time, the wealth gap between the wealthy and the general population grew wider than any other year.[6]

Regardless of how many promises politicians make and how many social programs politicians enact, wealth inequality will only increase.

---

[4] https://www.thebalance.com/average-credit-card-interest-rate-4772408
[5] https://en.wikipedia.org/wiki/Richard_Cantillon
[6] https://www.investopedia.com/2020-created-56-new-u-s-billionaires-5094234

Bailouts benefit the wealthy. Direct stimulus payments to people benefit the wealthy. Massive government spending benefits the wealthy.

It's not because someone is oppressing someone. It's because those who benefit understand the "Cantillon Effect" and the game of capital and wealth.

"We live on an economical planet, not a political planet." – Grant Cardone

Suppose you take all the capital and assets available on this planet and divide it equally between 7.8 billion people. I would wager that the wealthy will end up with approximately the same share within 12 months.

They have mastered the game of capital and wealth, while most people do not know that the game exists.

3) Personal Finance Basics, Financial Education, and Knowledge

Cashflow Ninjas also pointed out that people struggle financially because of the lack of education and knowledge regarding personal finance and their wealth.

Many highly educated people with university and college degrees and post-graduate and master's degrees struggle financially.

The main reason is that school and universities do not teach basic personal finance skills.

How is one supposed to independently manage their own capital and wealth without basic financial skills?

It is not in the interest of the people that created the game of capital and wealth and the rules of the game.

That is why students study photosynthesis, rather than learning how the global banking and financial system operates in educational institutions.

The education system in most countries is based on the Prussian School System[7], which was designed to produce workers and soldiers, not independent, creative, and critical thinkers.

Schools and universities are designed to produce employees and consumers.

Employees can work for major corporations and pay high taxes. They spend their remaining income to service their debt to banking and financial institutions and buy products and services from major corporations.

The paradigm of the majority of people only has them value academic education.

The wealthy value financial education. They value "street smarts" and not only "book smarts." It's no longer a jobs economy. It is a global marketplace that values skills.

Knowledge is not power. Power is the correct valuable knowledge applied to create and produce value in the global marketplace.

4) Data And Information

We live in a world overloaded with information and data. Never in the history of humanity have we had so much information accessible at our fingertips on our smartphones.

With more noise surrounding us than ever before, it is crucial to determine what data and information we consume and use to make decisions regarding our health, relationships, business, and wealth.

We have more financial and investment advisors and celebrities sharing information online than ever before. Yet, we have never had generations of people in worse financial situations.

---

[7] https://en.wikipedia.org/wiki/Prussian_education_system

When it comes to wealth in particular, 99% of the data, information, and advice is wrong and financially destructive, and dangerous.

Most people use this destructive and dangerous data, information, and advice without questioning it.

Why is 99% of the data, information, and advice published dangerous? Why would media platforms do this?

The media business model is remarkably simple.

Media companies try to drive as much traffic to their platforms to consume their content. In that way, advertisers would pay a lot of money for the opportunity to advertise to their large audience.

Fear, greed, and polarizing content that activates emotions drive traffic and get eyeballs and clicks.

The customers and clients of media platforms are the advertisers and sponsors, like Big Pharma (The Drug Dealers), The Military Industrial Complex (The War Profiteers), Big Tech and Data (The Surveillance Complex) and Wall Street (The Money Changers).

Selling drugs and war, gathering and selling consumer data, and skimming financial portfolios annually are very profitable ventures.

These corporations earn significant returns on their investment in advertising and public relations.

It is very profitable for them to continue to further their agendas through narratives pushed through media platforms.

So, what do the financial media (owned by corporations listed on stock exchanges and purchased by mutual fund managers), financial and personal finance celebrities, and financial advisors tell the majority of people to do?

Here's a hint: it mirrors what their advertisers, sponsors, and employers want them to do. Most people are unaware of this.

Most people are aware when they eat junk food but are not aware when they consume junk data and information, and fake news.

That is why most people struggle financially and constantly eat up dangerous and destructive narratives and horribly skewed biased data constantly without questioning anything.

"If you torture the data long enough, it will confess." – Ronald Coase

Banking and financial institutions, for example, want you to save and invest for the long term and not access your capital for a long time.

When you look at the business model of banking and financial institutions, you will understand why.

Robert Castiglione shared that the business model of banking and financial institutions is straightforward.

They want the capital of people, and they want it regularly.

Monthly or bi-weekly, preferably. They also prefer to take it directly from people's paychecks before they even have access to it.

The institutions are in control of the capital for as long as possible. When they give it back to people, they give back as little as possible and as slowly as possible.

Governments also love this model since you get to pay taxes on the harvest, not the seed. It greatly benefits them and allows them to collect more taxes.

Think of how your qualified retirement plans function.

So, what do you think the banking and financial institutions do when they receive your capital?

They collateralize and leverage it and then deploy it as soon as possible to create more capital through products that they create.

Banks' preferred method of doing so is lending, since banks can legally, through fractional reserve banking[8], lend more money than what they have on deposit.

They leverage debt, taxes and benefit from fees, interest, and inflation.

They are on the right side of the compound interest equation, while nearly everyone else is on the wrong side.

Banking and financial institutions, corporations, and the government benefit from the destructive data and information packaged and sold as advice to the masses.

If you are not paying for data and information, you are the product, not the customer or client.

Wealthy people pay for data and information, and the decisions are based on solid data and information.

The financial decision you will make will only be as good as the data and information you based your decision on.

That is why they make better decisions financially.

5) Wall Street's Plan Or An Aligned Strategy?

The media convinced most people that the management of their wealth needs to be outsourced to Wall Street.

They have also been sold Wall Street's plan of handing your capital over to a financial advisor. That person manages it for you and invests on your behalf for the long term in a diversified portfolio.

Most people give up all control of their capital. They have no idea what they are invested in and do not consider economic, market and asset cycles.

---

[8] https://en.wikipedia.org/wiki/Fractional-reserve_banking

There is no strategy and no tactical implementation and active management with the assistance of a wealth team.

The majority of people have been sold "The American Dream Financial Plan."

"It's called the American Dream because you have to be asleep to believe it." – George Carlin

The "American Dream Financial Plan," as packaged and sold to the public, is built entirely on HOPE.

When you go to university and college in 2021, the world you will enter four years later will be completely different from today.

University and college might not even be a thing in five years. They cannot prepare people for the rapidly disruptive marketplace we currently live in during the 4th Industrial Revolution.

It is not possible.

You are HOPING that what you learned, if anything, is still relevant.

You are HOPING you have a single skill that could get you a job.

You are HOPING jobs and employment still exist as they do today.

You are HOPING that you do not have a mountain of student loans to pay off.

You are HOPING you will be able to afford a house and all your student debt on your income. You are HOPING you will be able to save any capital for retirement.

You are HOPING that the capital you put in qualified savings vehicles and the capital you hand over to your financial advisor to manage for 30–40 years in a well-diversified portfolio of stocks, bonds and mutual funds will be a mountain of capital when you can retire, if ever.

You are HOPING that markets are at all-time highs when you need your capital to retire on. You are HOPING that your house is worth more and paid off when you retire.

You are HOPING that you have enough capital. You are also HOPING you can convert that capital into income through the Monte Carlo model that your financial advisor presented to you 30–40 years ago.

You are HOPING you die before you run out of capital.

The "American Dream Financial Plan" ONLY works when housing and equity markets go up. Not only is it 100% dependent on HOPE, but you have no CONTROL.

The wealthy have a strategy aligned with their life's vision and goals, their strengths, their individual and family investor DNA and investor profile. This leverages debt, the tax code, produces cash flow and enjoys the benefits of asset appreciation.

The strategy allows them to play the game of capital and wealth well and adjust when the rules of the game changes.

These wealthy individuals and families know that creating, building, and growing wealth does not need to be complicated.

You must have a skillset you can use to provide value to others in the economy to exchange for capital. Also, you need to spend less than you earn. You should save and invest the difference in assets that pay you to hold them, not liabilities. Also, you need to continue to save and re-invest for compounded growth.

While billionaires like Jeff Bezos are venturing into space, they are not defying gravity when it comes to wealth building.

They know how to play the game of capital and wealth.

They understand how banking and financial institutions, corporations and the government function.

They know that they created the game and the game board and have the power to change the rules and the game board at any time.

They know and understand the game's rules because they study the rule book, which is the tax code.

They bring in top experts and advisors, along with their coaches and mentors, to play on their wealth team to help them win.

Wealthy people adjust. It doesn't matter who is in political office and the state of the economy and in the markets. They adapt their strategies accordingly with their wealth team and continue to build their wealth.

The wealthy study the best players in the game of capital and wealth and play the game in the current environment, not the environment they wished existed.

Wealthy people do not do the same as everyone else. They do not just do something different. They do the complete opposite.

They are not interested in averages. They are not interested in average lives. They focus on building a bigger and better future daily and are pursuing *exceptional* lives.

"You can be conventional, or you can be wealthy. Pick one." – Dave Zook

I have studied multi-millionaires, billionaires, and successful entrepreneurs, business owners and investors for close to two decades. I have also interviewed over 700 top wealth creators on my podcast, Cashflow Ninja. This enabled me to create a model and framework that Cashflow Ninjas utilize to play the game of capital and wealth.

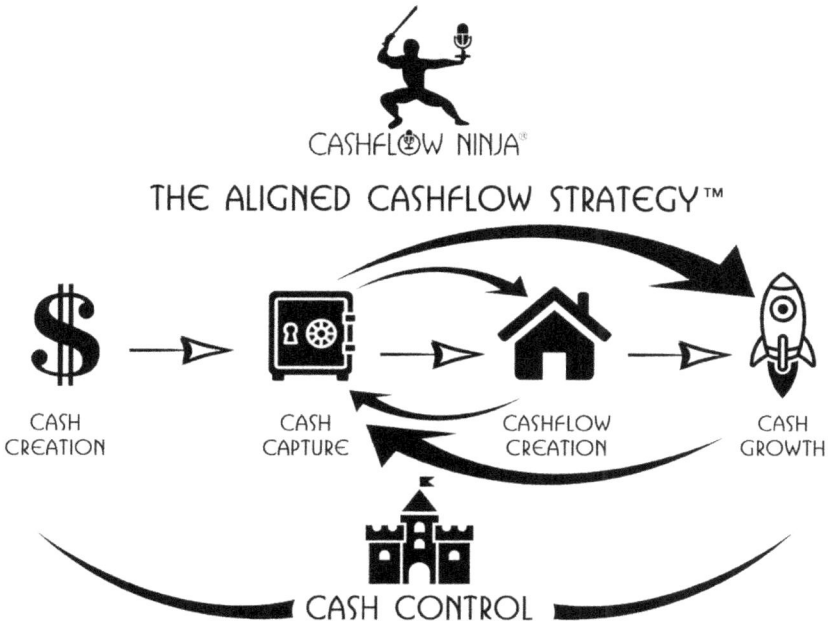

CASHFLOW NINJA®

THE ALIGNED CASHFLOW STRATEGY™

| CASH CREATION | CASH CAPTURE | CASHFLOW CREATION | CASH GROWTH |

CASH CONTROL

Cashflow Ninjas strategically align their resources to grow their capital and wealth daily and intentionally.

The framework consists of five pillars: cash creation, cash capture, cash flow creation, cash growth and cash control.

The cash creation pillar is where Cashflow Ninjas create capital by creating value for the marketplace through their businesses. They do this by producing products and services that solve problems and achieve desirable outcomes. The result of the value creation is the exchange of capital for their products and services.

The more value that is created in the marketplace, the more capital is created.

In cash capture, wealth creators and producers position the capital efficiently and effectively.

Before capital can be properly collateralized and leveraged to create more capital, it must first be efficiently warehoused and protected. Cash capture protects the capital created from wealth destroyers such as taxes, inflation, fees, creditors, and opportunity costs.

Within cash capture, Cashflow Ninjas establish their own bank and banking system to become their own source of financing.

At the cash flow creation, Cashflow Ninjas deploy the capital in assets that produce cash flow and appreciate in value.

This is the process where Cashflow Ninjas will multiply their cash by using carefully crafted cash flow investing strategies.

These Cashflow Ninjas invest for cash flow to create income streams from real estate, paper assets, commodities, businesses, and cryptocurrencies.

In this book, I will share 21 of the best cash flow niches that Cashflow Ninjas have discovered.

The cash growth pillar is the part of the framework where capital is positioned to achieve explosive growth. Investments in technology and technology businesses have been a great area to invest for explosive growth.

The cash control pillar helps Cashflow Ninjas protect what they have produced, created, and built.

Cashflow Ninjas establish a solid tax strategy and bulletproof asset protection and estate plan through proper cash control.

Through this framework, Cashflow Ninjas own the businesses that buy real estate. Through proper cash flow management structuring, they create their own banking system.

What Is Cash Flow Investing?

Most people buy assets and hope they go up in value. They hope that they accumulate enough assets to eventually "retire" over 30–40 years. There is another strategy that enables you to become financially independent and self-reliant much sooner.

Cash flow investing is a strategy where one invests in assets like real estate, businesses, paper assets, commodities, and cryptocurrencies to generate income from the investment immediately.

Through cash flow investing, you are acquiring an asset that pays you to own it.

Instead of working for capital, cash flow investing has your capital working for you and producing more capital in the process.

Through cash flow investing, you will find out quickly if the investment and the strategy are working or not, and you can adjust or even cut your losses short.

You don't have to wait 30–40 years to see if the investment or strategy worked.

When done strategically, you can generate an income stream from an asset class regardless of whether markets go up, down, sideways, or whether the economy is in a boom or bust.

With cash flow investing, instead of trying to accumulate enough capital by trading 30–40 years of your time, you will free up your time in exchange for the capital invested.

Through cash flow investing, one asset investment can pay you for the rest of your life.

Passive Income, earned through cash flow investing, also receives the most favorable tax treatment.

Earned income and portfolio income (capital gains), generated from the accumulation model, are taxed much higher.

The goal of cash flow investors is to achieve freedom, independence, and self-reliance today, rather than waiting for retirement.

Cash flow investors know that retirement isn't freedom. It's part of the "American Dream Financial Plan" scheme and marketing pitch.

Cash flow investors can become financially independent and self-reliant when they have more income from cash flow investments than their current living expenses.

How quickly can you achieve freedom through cash flow investing?

It will be different for everyone depending on your assets, resources, and income. Still, anyone can achieve financial independence and freedom regardless of age, income, and current financial condition.

Through cash flow investing, you own the goose that lays the golden eggs, and you collect the eggs. You can diversify your portfolio of golden geese by owning many geese that provide many golden eggs.

While most people buy their goose and cook it, Cashflow Ninjas own the goose to collect the eggs.

A New Definition Of Wealth

The financial media and celebrities have convinced 99% of the world that the way to measure wealth is by looking at what you have accumulated. This is also known as your net worth, or statement wealth.

The wealthy know that your net worth does not matter. The value of your businesses and assets is important. However, it is the cash flow of your businesses and assets that matters most.

They understand that if they focus on cash flow and increase the cash flow from their businesses and investments, the value of these assets will appreciate.

By focusing on cash flow and increasing cash flow that increases the value of your assets, your net worth will continue to increase as well.

For that reason, they focus on contractual wealth, not statement wealth.

Robert Kiyosaki is the author of the best-selling personal finance book *Rich Dad, Poor Dad*. He wrote that the new way to determine wealth is to answer the following question:

"If you stop working today, how long will you be able to maintain your current standard of living?"

One of the biggest wealth secrets you won't hear from financial media and celebrities is that wealth is measured in time, not net worth.

If your answer was one year, you have the wealth you need to live for one year.

If instead, you answered that you could maintain your current lifestyle for the rest of your life, you are infinitely wealthy.

You can passively generate the monthly income from your investments through cash flow investing strategies – and never outlive your capital.

Additionally, you can transfer these cash flow generating assets to your children and your children's children.

Cash flow investing will allow you to build and live your legacy today and leave a legacy for your family.

Reverse Engineering Wealth

Why do people die?

Other than health deterioration, multiple studies suggest that people die when they lose purpose in their life, they lose relationships, or when they run out of money.

So, if you think about wealth, then the four reasons people die are also the four things that allow us to live life to the fullest and fulfill our potential as people on this earth.

My definition of wealth is to have age-defying health, soulful and fulfilling relationships, daily dedication to my purpose and legacy, and infinite cash flow income streams from my businesses and investments.

Cash flow investing is a strategy that can help you achieve that.

If you have passive income each month, quarter, and year that can support the life of your dreams, regardless of how you spend your time, you are truly free.

Free to spend your time as you choose, with the people you choose to, while focusing on your purpose and projects that you are passionate about.

How Can You Get Started With Cash Flow Investing?

You can invest as an active or passive investor. There are advantages and disadvantages to both.

Active Investing

As an active investor, you will play a significant, hands-on role in the performance of the investment, whether it is the identification, acquisition, management, or sale of the business or property.

Suppose you locate and buy a distressed single-family property, rehab, and fix up the property. Then, you rent it to a tenant from whom you collect monthly rent (and field maintenance calls). You're an active investor.

Active investments allow you to have full control over the entire process. The success of the investment is based on your knowledge and expertise to find the property, and your capital and credit to buy it. It is also based on your team and network to rehab the property, and your management expertise to find and screen the tenant and continue to deal with management issues.

If you hand this investment property off to a management company, it would still be considered an active investment since the property manager would report to you.

The success of the investment is completely dependent on your intellectual capital, skill sets and capabilities, financial capital, and your team and network.

This will limit how many of these investments you can make and how quickly you can make them.

Passive Investing

The second way to invest for cash flow is to invest as a passive investor.

Let's face it. No investment is truly passive. It might be passive for you, but it is not passive for someone else.

You leverage another person's skills sets and capabilities, knowledge, unique ability, resources, and networks through passive investing. You provide the capital for the investment, and the other person and or party does the rest.

I prefer to look at this type of investing as leveraged investing, but it is widely known as passive investing.

Through passive investing, you can find a company that identifies and finds properties, brings in their own team to rehab the property, finds and screens the tenant, and then manages the property for you on a fee basis.

As the passive investor, you receive a monthly check from the company that provides the service for you.

As a passive investor, you can also invest in real estate by purchasing passive shares of an LLC (a Limited Liability Corporation). This is managed by an operator who oversees the entire investment process. For the value that the operator provides, they receive partial ownership of the LLC.

With both passive investment examples, the operator's only communication with the passive investor is providing basic property information, answering questions, and sending quarterly reports outlining the performance of the property.

Being a passive investor allows investors to profit from an extremely experienced company or operator's time, expertise, relationships, credit, and assumption of liability.

As a passive investor, you do not need to become specialized in an investment niche to invest since you can partner with companies and operators that are specialized.

This allows you to diversify your cash flow investments within several markets, as you can create numerous advantageous relationships and partnerships quickly.

Besides leveraging the intellectual and relationship capital of others, you are also leveraging the credit and capital of others in syndications. As a passive investor in an LLC, you can eliminate liability exposure.

In 2001, I jumped into action and bought my first real estate investment property as an active investor.

After the tenant paid the rent and I deducted the mortgage, taxes, insurance, vacancy allowance, and assessments, there was capital left. I received my first monthly cash flow from my real estate investment.

This was the biggest "Ah-ha!" moment of my life. It was like I discovered the Holy Grail of investing.

My thoughts leaped to, "How many of these deals can I do?"

I learned many valuable, hard lessons and lost capital in some of my active investments. Then I started partnering with operators that were at the top of their game, specialized in their field, and operating within their zone of genius.

I started as an active investor and transitioned to a passive investor by investing in syndications.

As a passive investor, you can research the different asset classes and niches within the asset classes. You can research the asset cycles and research market cycles within the different asset classes and niches. You can research and interview investment operators, ask them about their investment strategies and see if that is aligned with your investor DNA and within your risk profile.

I have spent many hours finding the best operators in the best niches that I want to invest in. This time investment has allowed me to have deal flow of the best investment opportunities from the best operators with strategies aligned with me as an investor.

I share this deal flow and monthly asset class presentations with my community of accredited investors in the Cashflow Ninja Cashflow Investors Club™.

To learn more, you can visit www.cashflowninja.com/club.

What are some of the best cash flow investing niches that I have had Cashflow Ninjas share on my podcast, Cashflow Ninja?

There have been many and, in this book, I will share the 21 best cash flow niches shared on my show.

It was tough to narrow it down to 21, so I included five bonus niches for you to enjoy! The niches are in no specific order.

I hope these 21 cash flow niches and five bonus niches serve as a launchpad for your cash flow investing journey.

Niche #1: Businesses

From starting and growing to owning and selling, businesses have long been the primary vehicle for wealth creation for multi-millionaires and billionaires.

80% of millionaires today are self-made millionaires[9]. The majority of the new millionaires did so by starting and growing a business.

Businesses today are categorized as brick-and-mortar businesses or online businesses. However, every business should have an online presence. Today, businesses operate 24 hours a day, 7 days a week, 365 days per year.

You can actively start a business through a side hustle while you are still working like many very successful people have done. You grow that business until you can leave your job and pursue the business full-time.

The richest man in the world, Jeff Bezos, worked on Wall Street when he started selling a non- perishable product that could sit in a warehouse for a long time. This business, Amazon, started with books.

Steve Jobs coded computer games at Atari, and Steve Wozniak worked at IBM when they started Apple Computers part-time.

Daymond John, known affectionately as "the people's shark" and founder/owner of FUBU, worked at Red Lobster when he started his business.

Apart from a side hustle business, you can dive right in and start your full-time business if you can do so.

---

[9] https://spendmenot.com/blog/what-percentage-of-americans-are-millionaires/

Many resources, including books, courses, and podcasts share information on starting a business. Since it is not the main focus of this book, I will not discuss starting a business. I will share a framework that aspiring entrepreneurs and investors in businesses can utilize.

If you are interested to learn how to start a business and grow that business, you can join our program, The Cashflow Creator Formula ™ at www.cashflowninja.com/creator.

The framework I use to brainstorm and analyze potential business opportunities is as follow:

1) Is value provided? How is value provided?

2) Who is being served?

3) Is there a market? How big is the market?

4) How unique is the delivery and process of transformation?

5) Who are the operators, investors, team and management?

Is Value Provided?

There are only two reasons for businesses to exist. A business should solve a problem or create and deliver a desired outcome through products and services.

People find themselves in their current situation, and they would like to achieve a desired situation.

I learned from Sam Ovens that you create value in the marketplace if you can help people go from their current situation to their desired situation through your products and services.

If you are starting a business and the business does not take someone from their current situation to their desired situation through your products and services, you will end up being another statistic.

If you invest in a business that tries to create value in this manner, your capital investment is gone!

So, when brainstorming business ideas and looking for investment opportunities, look at what problems are being solved and what desirable outcomes could be achieved.

Who is Being Served?

Who are you looking to serve? What part of the market are you looking to serve?

Be very clear on who you are trying to serve and what part of the market you are serving.

I learned a great example from J Massey of the three stores: Nordstrom, Target and Walmart.

They all sell shirts and make money selling shirts, but to different markets. Nordstrom serves higher-income customers. Target serves the middle class and Walmart, the lower-income customers.

All three stores make money selling shirts, but they have identified their niches.

Is There A Market? How Big?

Three areas in our lives have challenges that people desire to transform into something more favorable.

Those three areas are health, relationships, and wealth. Inside these three markets are dozens of sub-markets.

Health: Nutrition, Diet, Strength Training, Weight Loss, etc.

Relationships: Love, Dating Advice, Marriage Advice, Family Counseling, etc.

Wealth: Finance, Investing, Real Estate, Sales, Cryptocurrencies, etc.

Inside these markets and sub-markets, you will be able to find your niche. And inside the niches, you will find more niches.

How big is the market in which you will start your business or invest in a business?

How Unique Is The Delivery And Process Of Transformation?

How unique are your products and services that solve the problem and create outcomes for the identified market? Is your business different?

Are you competing in a red ocean full of sharks? Will you just be another business in that niche?

Can you create your own market within that niche through your business so that you're operating in a blue ocean?

If you have a unique delivery, process, or elegant solution, the chance of success is higher. Let's look at Uber as an example of a unique delivery, process and elegant solution.

People disliked taking taxis. Not only were they impersonal, but hailing a cab could be nearly impossible in busy cities during busy times. In small towns, taxis were practically non-existent.

Once you're in a taxi, you often realize they're dirty or smell bad. You can rarely determine the cost from point A to point B, and the payment options are restrictive. The list goes on, but the taxi system was practically begging to be reformed.

Uber created an elegant solution many people's problems by creating a ride-share application on your smartphone.

You can go to the Uber app and order a ride that will pick you up at your location and drop you off at your destination, all while knowing the cost upfront. Uber also eliminated the need for a money exchange since your card on file will pay for the ride.

The best part? You're practically guaranteed a clean, maintained vehicle since drivers use personal cars and depend on good ratings. These same ratings help you know what to expect from your driver or your passenger.

This free-market mechanism ensures that horrible drivers will limit their clientele, and horrible passengers will struggle to find drivers willing to transport them.

Uber does not own any cars and does not employ any drivers directly. It's a technology company.

Who Are The Operators, Investors, Team and Management?

Do you have the skills, competency, and capability, or do you need to partner? Do you need capital from investors? Who do you need to be part of your team?

If you are a potential investor, the operators, investors, team and management will be instrumental to the business's success.

Once you have started your business and created your products and services that solve a problem or create a desired outcome, you can build out a value ladder of products and services and create a network of dream partners and affiliates to distribute your product or service.

Starting a business might sound risky to many people. It might also sound risky investing in a startup business or getting involved as an investor during the early stages.

The Small Business Administration (SBA) states that 30% of new businesses fail during the first two years after opening, 50% during the first five years, and 66% during the first 10.[10]

This risk does not align with the wealth creation or investor DNA of most people. So, there are several other options available to create cash flow in business.

One remedy is to buy an existing established business. The proprietary assets like their products and services, systems and processes, and their client/customer lists alleviate some risks. The company might have a great brand or reputation as well.

---

[10] https://www.sba.gov/sites/default/files/Business-Survival.pdf

Often, you can negotiate with the seller of a business to stay on for a period until you feel comfortable with the transition.

If you buy a business, you can do so as an active owner, working in the business daily, or as a passive owner with a manager who runs the business for you.

Carl Allen shared that rather than starting a business from scratch or merely maintaining an existing business, you can also look at buying a business in your niche. You can then launch your personal product or service though an established business.

The benefit here would be that you already have a profitable business with a customer and or client base to sell your new product and or service.

This strategy provides stable and predictable cash flow, access to a customer and or client list, and access to already established partnerships and business systems.

If your product or service fails, you still have a stable business providing cash flow. Without the established business, you're left with a failed product or service and wasted time and resources.

You can also buy, as an active or passive investor, a franchise. Buying a franchise brings the brand, regional and national footprint, and a business system all in one.

This is a great choice for those who want to work with a company with an established business model and systems. Plus, they'll often provide the training you need to be successful.

If you want to start a business with a minimal barrier of entry (usually a couple hundred bucks), join a network marketing or multi-level marketing company.

Yes, I am going to go there. Your family and friends and Facebook friends are wrong about network marketing and multi-level marketing.

Here's why.

Network marketing companies focus on growing and developing the people inside of their companies. The personal development and training you will receive for joining the company for a couple of hundred bucks is better than any education you receive in an MBA program.

I know because I attended network marketing training and personal development events with my mother in the early 2000s and completed my MBA. I learned FAR more about business from these training sessions than in my MBA program.

Network marketing organizations will also assign you a mentor to help you build your business, just like it works in the real business world. And the mentors assigned to you have real-life success, unlike a professor teaching in the MBA program that has never started or grown a business.

Generating cash flow through a business has never been more accessible to anyone with internet connection. You can start a business, online business, e-commerce business, buy an existing business, buy a franchise, or join a network marketing company,

During massive societal and global changes and paradigm shifts, entrepreneurs capitalize on massive opportunities.

Fortunes were made during economic and market crashes, world wars, and the Great Depression. And many millionaires and billionaires were created in 2020.

We are currently living during the 4th Industrial Revolution and The Great Reset. This new global environment will continue to experience massive changes, disruptions, and chaos.

There are emerging trends that entrepreneurs and investors can capitalize on to position themselves to be on the right side of the greatest wealth transfer in human history.

One of the biggest opportunities that I see for entrepreneurs right now is e-commerce businesses.

The e-commerce share of total retail sales in the United States in 2021 is currently only at 13.6%.[11]

If you think you missed the opportunity to start an e-commerce business, you could not be more wrong.

This is just the beginning. This trend will continue to accelerate.

One of the biggest opportunities of our time is starting your own drop-shipping, e-commerce or Amazon business.

Any brick-and-mortar business can also replicate online what they are doing offline through the technology available in 2021.

The cryptocurrency and blockchain technology space is another opportunity and industry that is poised to change the world, just like the rollout of the internet did in the late 1990s and early 2000s.

Entrepreneurs can start businesses in this space, and investors can invest directly in businesses.

A great opportunity exists through implementing a "California gold rush" strategy. During the California gold rush in 1849, fortunes were not made by the people that dug and panned for gold. Instead, fortunes were made by the people that sold picks, shovels, equipment, food, clothes, housing, financial services and entertainment to the fortune seekers that came to California.

Entrepreneurs and investors that missed the opportunity to invest in dotcom startups, like Google and Amazon, now have a second opportunity to invest in a niche that will disrupt every business on the planet.

---

[11] https://www.statista.com/statistics/187439/share-of-e-commerce-sales-in-total-us-retail-sales-in-2010/

The Pros Of Businesses

Being a business owner gives you independence. Dan Sullivan, shares that by becoming an entrepreneur or business owner, you have relinquished society from supporting and taking care of you.

You will have to create value for the market place in exchange for capital. You have full control, including over your income, expenses, and debt.

You can leverage the time, money, skill sets, capabilities, and expertise of other people through owning your business.

There is no limit to how much revenue you and your company can make. Being a business owner, you can benefit greatly from the tax law.

Most of the tax law, in most countries, is geared toward reducing the taxes of business owners. If you are investing in businesses, you also have tax advantages as an investor.

You set your own hours and choose what you are working on. You have the freedom to express yourself fully, who you are and what you stand for through your business.

You don't even have to re-invent the wheel, as you can buy an existing business or franchise instead of building one from scratch. You buy proven business system, processes, proprietary assets, existing customer and client lists, established partnerships, and affiliate partners.

Entrepreneurship is a lifelong personal development course. There is no better teacher than doing. You can even start your own business for very little investment by joining a network marketing group to learn.

The Cons Of Businesses

Starting, building, and growing a business is one of the hardest things to do, and that is why so few people do it.

Running a business or franchise you bought is not easy either and requires leadership and managerial skills.

There is also a high failure rate. The Small Business Administration (SBA) states that 30% of new businesses fail during the first two years after opening, 50% during the first five years, and 66% during the first 10.

You have to work long hours. This isn't a 9–5 job – you will likely work nights, weekends and holidays.

There is no guarantee of a steady paycheck or any income.

You must deal with and manage employees, clients, consultants, vendors, etc., along with their various personalities and moods. This can be quite stressful if you don't enjoy this work.

Investing in new businesses can be risky because there is a high failure rate. Venture capitalists expect that one out of ten businesses they invest in, will be a successful investment. They accept that nine out of ten businesses they invest in, will fail.

<u>Niche #2: Turnkey Real Estate</u>

Residential turnkey real estate is an excellent way for investors to passively invest in residential real estate without the headaches of an active investor.

Residential turnkey real estate includes single-family homes, and 2 to 4-unit properties.

Turnkey real estate companies sell new or fully renovated properties seasoned with tenants and managed by a property management company.

An active investor has to find properties to buy, rehab, fix them up, then find and screen suitable tenants. Then, they are responsible for managing the property, fielding phone calls for maintenance requests, and more.

A turnkey real estate investment company does all of this for you. You, as the investor, are only involved when receiving periodic updates on your property and whether there are major decisions to be made regarding your property.

Turnkey companies make their money by buying a property at a discount and rehabbing it, then selling it at a retail price to investors. They then receive a management fee for managing your property on your behalf.

Investors invest in single-family real estate for the cash flow, property appreciation, and amortization of your mortgage with your tenants paying down the mortgage for you, and tax benefits like depreciation.

When you buy a property, the physical structure of the house/building and all fixtures actually get older and deteriorate – although the value of the property increases.

Taxes can also be indefinitely deferred on the sale of the property through 1031 exchanges.

Consider, too, that real estate is an effective hedge against inflation since you have control over the rent. You can leverage the bank's money to acquire the asset, and then leverage that property (through leveraging the equity) to acquire another one, and so on.

Real estate offers a wide array of benefits without the need for much active participation.

The Pros Of Turnkey Real Estate

Turnkey real estate is very convenient for passive investors.

You do not have to actively look and search to find properties, saving your most valuable resource: time. You can leverage the turnkey provider's network and ability to find great rental properties in the market that they know really well.

You don't have to rehab and fix up the property yourself. You can leverage the team and skill set of the turnkey operators to fix up the properties. You don't have to manage contractors. You can also leverage the operator's economies of scale to buy materials at a discount because of the volume of materials they purchase.

You can leverage the network and Rolodex of the turnkey provider for mortgage lenders, insurance professionals, and other team members you might need as part of your team.

You do not have to manage the property. You do not have to find tenants and screen them, collect rent, send reminders and late notices, and deal with evictions. You also do not have to deal with any maintenance calls and coordinate maintenance services.

You can start collecting rent immediately. Since there is usually a tenant in place before you close on the home, you can start collecting rental income when you finalize the purchase.

Turnkey real estate allows investors to diversify in more than one market without being an expert in the market. Investors can own properties all over the United States without ever setting foot in one of them.

Some turnkey markets are great cash flow markets, and some are great appreciation markets. You can diversify into both these markets through turnkey real estate investing.

Turnkey providers can provide certain guarantees like rent, vacancy, and more.

You do not have to be an accredited investor. It is not necessary to have a lot of capital to get started in turnkey real estate.

The Cons Of Turnkey Real Estate

Not all turnkey providers that market themselves as such are turnkey providers. Anyone that has researched this niche or invested in it will know that many operators do not manage the process from start to finish.

A true turnkey operator will provide an experience where you simply put in your key and turn the key to unlock the investment.

The operator will find the property, rehab and fix it, find a suitable tenant, and manage the property for you after closing. That is what a turnkey experience should be like.

You also still need to go through the process of being a real estate investor. You need to research the market, have a checklist for your desired properties, and do your due diligence on turnkey operators, the properties itself, and more.

Like any business, you need to understand who you are going to serve as an investor.

Properties that sell for $40,000 are much different than properties that sell for $75,000 or $120,000. Each of these price points has different neighborhoods, different tenants, and other variables.

It is very important to understand this, otherwise there will be a lot of surprises. When much is left to surprise, you'll be left with an unpleasant experience in the best case. In the worst case, you'll be stuck with an investment that loses you capital.

When buying a turnkey property, you will pay a retail price for your property. You will not buy the property at a discounted price. Make sure you buy at or below market value.

When you have one turnkey property and one vacancy, you have a 100% vacancy. With 1–4 units, the vacancy rate can be very high, and one vacancy can have a very big impact on your cash flow.

With turnkey real estate investing, the property's price is also tied to the market. So, you cannot force price appreciation through operations and value-added management strategies.

This is real estate, and you assume real estate risks, like bad tenants that do not pay rent, damage your property, and more.

Niche #3: Multifamily Real Estate

Investing in multifamily real estate is one of the most powerful investments available to investors. The wealthy have warehoused their wealth in commercial real estate for a long time.

Affordable, clean, and livable housing is constantly in demand, and real estate investors get to provide this to the marketplace.

Multifamily real estate is a building or structure designed to house several different families in separate housing units. The most common type of multifamily housing is apartment buildings.

Apartment buildings can be categorized into four different classes.

A-class apartments are the newest and shiniest apartments and represent the highest quality in the market. Newer buildings under five years of age contain amenities catering to white-collar workers.

B-class apartments are a step down from A-class apartments. They are built in the last 20 years and cater to a mix of white- and blue-collar workers. The property may show a bit of deferred maintenance. Overall, this class has a good mix of cash flow and appreciation.

C-class apartments were built within the last 25 years or more and have deferred maintenance issues. These are often located in more difficult areas and generally need big capital expenditure investments, like a roof, to remain competitive in the rental market.

D-class apartments are the lowest class of the properties. These are more difficult to collect rent from and more difficult to exit the deal. However, D-class apartments can produce great cash flow for headaches and trouble.

Each of these apartment classes offer different challenges but can provide affordable housing for different types of tenants.

Just as with single-family real estate, there are several reasons investors invest in multifamily real estate. They invest for the cash flow, the appreciation of the property's value, amortization of the mortgage, and tax benefits like cost segregation and depreciation.

Depreciation is when the property's value and personal property go down and can be written off through taxes.

Taxes can also be indefinitely deferred on the sale of the property through 1031 exchanges, and multifamily real estate is a great hedge against inflation since you can increase the rent.

Another advantage is the ability to leverage the bank's money and the money from investors to acquire the asset, then leverage one property to acquire another through collateralizing the equity. You can do this for example through a cash-out refinance.

When operators refinance the multifamily property, they return the original capital of investors, which is not taxable, and investors still enjoy cash flow from the investment. The investors can then invest in another multifamily property and do this process again, thereby increasing the velocity and movement of their money.

You can also invest in multifamily and commercial real estate as a passive investor through syndications. A real estate syndication is a means for multiple investors to pull funds together to invest in larger commercial real estate deals.

An operator (general partner) has some money in the deal, but primarily contributes knowledge, experience, relationships, systems, and processes. The investors (limited partners) finance the deal in exchange for a return on their investments.

A pro of investing in multifamily real estate syndication is that the investment is hands-off. You receive passive and residual income, for which there are great tax benefits.

A con of investing in multifamily real estate syndication is that you have very little control over the investment. The money you invested is not liquid and is tied up within the investment for a period.

The main driver of the multifamily investment success is the operator.

Although it is real estate, the investment is all about the people involved. Great operators will have great partners, team members, and a great management team.

Other main drivers of real estate success are the markets that properties are located in that are driven by demographics and employer base.

If many people are moving into the markets you are considering, and there are many companies from diverse industries providing jobs, there will be an increasing demand for housing.

Consequently, if people are leaving the markets and employers are leaving as well, it is not going to be a good market to invest in.

Besides the operator, market demographics, and employment trends, other factors to consider when evaluating deals are the purchase information (i.e., purchase price, cost of rehab, etc.), financing details (i.e., loan amount, down payment, interest rate, closing costs, etc.), income, expenses, cash flow, rates of return (return on investment, cash-on-cash, internal rate of return, etc.) and capitalization rate (cap rate).

The Pros Of Multifamily Real Estate

Multifamily investments provide great, stable cash flow if purchased and managed correctly.

There are many symbiotic income streams on properties besides rent. Other sources of income can be pet deposits/rental fees, storage fees, parking, and more.

In multifamily real estate, your tenants can help with amortizing your mortgages. They pay down the mortgage's principal and increase the equity in the building. You are growing your equity in the property through leverage.

Since you can control the value through management strategies, you can control equity in the property.

You can force appreciation of the multifamily property through management, operations, and value-add strategies.

The value from commercial real estate is determined by dividing the net operating income by the capitalization rate. The net operating income is the net income generated by the property. The capitalization rate is an estimate of the investor's potential return on their investment in the real estate market.

The capitalization rate is determined by dividing the net operating income by the market value. You can find a market's cap rate by calling appraisers, brokers and looking at cap rates of comparable properties in your market.

If you can control and increase the net operating income, you can control the property's value and increase your property's value.

Tax benefits of depreciation and cost segregation.

Cost segregation is a process of identifying personal property, assets that are grouped with real property assets, and separating out personal assets for tax reporting purposes. When buying a multifamily building, assets such as hot water heaters, air conditioning units, and refrigerators are segregated out of the building itself and then reclassified. This strategy will accelerate depreciation and legally reduce your taxes.

You can defer taxes indefinitely when selling apartment buildings through 1031 strategies.

Multifamily real estate is a great hedge against inflation since you can pass on inflated costs through increased rents.

This strategy provides the opportunity to leverage the money of investors and the bank to finance the investment. You then use the investment to acquire other investments by refinancing the property and pulling out the equity after increasing the value of the property. The equity is accessed tax-free in this strategy, and you can use the equity to buy another investment.

Multifamily investments are easier to scale since you can buy multiple units, 5, 10, or 100 units, with one transaction. There might be more variables involved with purchasing a multifamily property than buying a single-family unit. With the same energy level you can essentially buy 100 units as opposed to one house.

You can diversify and spread your risk over more units with multifamily buildings.

Managing a multifamily building of 50–100 units is much easier than managing a portfolio of the same size in single-family real estate investments. It is simply far easier to have eight, 10 or even 50 tenants all in one location than dealing with the same number of tenants spread out over a large geographic area. Not to mention with a large number of units in the same locale, you increase your negotiation power with your property manager.

With multifamily investing, you tap into the power of economies of scale. You can have one mortgage, insurance policy, and property manager for 100 units, versus one house.

When you purchase a single-family property, you have to qualify on your own for the mortgage. When you buy a multifamily building, the loan qualification is based more on the investment (the building) than all of your own personal assets and liabilities. It is a much easier and smoother loan process because the asset is collateral for the loan. With a single-family home, your ability to earn income and pay for the home is the collateral.

The Cons Of Multifamily Real Estate

There are more barriers to entry in multifamily and commercial real estate in general.

There is higher price point, so you need more money to get into the game than you do with single-family real estate. Multifamily buildings cost a lot more than single-family properties for active investors.

You cannot compete as an active investor with the professionals starting part-time. You're competing against Cashflow Ninjas with professional teams playing at a very high level.

When you're a beginner, it is very hard to compete with established investors. They have networks, buying power, and a track record, to find the best operators and sponsors in every market and partner with them.

Most multifamily real estate syndications only allow accredited investors.

Investing in multifamily properties is more complicated from a legal perspective. More regulations surround multi-family properties. You should make a legal team member a priority when you consider actively investing in multifamily properties.

Niche #4: Hospitality Investing

Most of us have stayed in short-term rental accommodations, hotels, and resorts while traveling for work or vacations.

There is an incredible business side to the hospitality industry, and I will share with you two of the best cash flow opportunities I see in the hospitality industry today.

The first is the incredible opportunity currently for real estate entrepreneurs in the sharing economy.

Home share services like Airbnb and VRBO have taken the hospitality industry by storm. They have, to an extent, disrupted the hospitality industry in such a way that cities and states in the United States had to pass laws to protect the short-term rental industry.

On services like Airbnb and VRBO, people can list rooms, apartments, condos, and houses that they own for short-term rental accommodations to visitors in their towns and cities. It has become a reliable source of income for a lot of property owners.

One of the greatest business models I have seen is where real estate entrepreneurs have moved into the short-term rental space. They have created businesses that rent rooms, apartments, condos and houses that they DO NOT OWN but control on Airbnb and VRBO.

Real estate entrepreneurs contact owners of apartments, condos and homes. They negotiate with them to either lease their apartments, condos and houses or split the revenue that they generate renting the rooms, apartments, condos and houses on Airbnb and VRBO.

The property owners get their real estate leased and receive rent on the properties they own. They also have a tenant that professionally cleans their property every week and does not bother them with any maintenance or other annoying requests.

The real estate entrepreneurs take control over the real estate, furnish the properties and lists them for rent as short-term rentals on Airbnb and VRBO.

They then systemize the process of finding properties, controlling them, listing the short-term rentals, and professionally cleaning and turning over the properties for the next guest. They have virtual assistance to manage the systems.

For the most part, real estate is leased and priced long term, and there is a massive demand for short-term quality rentals. This market inefficiency is a fantastic area that entrepreneurs are exploiting. Because of that, they are building very profitable businesses in this niche.

For more information on this specific strategy, you can watch a presentation at www.cashflowninja.com/luxuryrentals.

The resort niche of hospitality is another business model and opportunity in hospitality about which I am super excited. I personally invest in this niche.

While franchised hotel brands are the most recognizable names in the hospitality industry, over 60% of hotels and resorts are independently owned and operated.

This is also where one of the greatest opportunities in the hospitality niche lies: the opportunity to invest in independently owned and managed world-class resorts.

The strategy involves buying historic, trophy, distressed resort properties needing some TLC with an interesting history, character and soul. Then, you turn them into fully functioning, highly profitable, and gorgeous resorts.

These properties are located close to major markets and big cities.

There are higher profit margins and returns by investing in fix and hold lifestyle investment properties instead of buying into already up-and-running resorts.

Josh and Melanie McCallen call this the BRRR (buy, rehab, rent, refinance, and repeat) strategy for resorts.

A unique property with history, character, and soul, distressed from delayed maintenance or neglect at an attractive price, is a diamond in the rough.

With an opportunity to be redeveloped while maintaining the character and soul of the resort, you hold an enormous business opportunity.

You can access symbiotic and complementary revenue streams while you implement and execute the BRRR strategy.

Weddings are the number one most efficient way to add highly profitable revenue and ultimately explode a resort's net operating income.

You can also add festival and event programming that allows loyal guests to return more often, thus lowering guest acquisition costs.

Adding resort fees that can be collected in resorts include added amenities that produce value for the guests, turning traditional operational expenses into profit centers.

Resorts are cash flow machines on steroids because of all the symbiotic and ancillary revenue stream opportunities it provides.

One of the resort projects I am a partner and investor in is the historic Renault and Winery Resort in southern New Jersey, about 25 minutes outside Atlantic City.

It is situated where guests can reach it easily from several airports. It is also favorably positioned to get many visitors and guests from New

York, Philadelphia, and other major cities on the east coast. These Guests can access the resort without having to board a plane.

Renault is the third oldest winery in the United States and has a rich and unique history.

It is one of the very few wineries outside the Champagne province in France that can produce champagne and call it "American Champagne." The Renault champagne was also served at the presidential inauguration of John F. Kennedy.

The property is famous for characters visiting the winery over the past 150 years like Joe Kennedy, Al Capone, and many famous organized crime characters.

There was a lot of alcohol production during prohibition on that 250 acres of land.

Renault has a winery golf course, hotel, restaurant, and several wedding venues. Besides the winery, it also has a full liquor license.

Weddings are the main revenue driver, but the complementary and symbiotic cash flow streams at the resort are incredible.

People book their weddings at the resort. Family and friends stay at the hotel, eat at the restaurants, play golf during the day, relax at the winery's tasting room, and then enjoy the wedding at one of the wedding venues. The property can host four weddings simultaneously. There is also a speak-easy after-party venue.

The property is only 50% of what determines the satisfaction of guest experience in the hospitality industry. The other 50% is based on the staff and people at the resort.

As with all real estate and business investments, the success is based on the people involved, the operator, the team, the management and the resort staff.

One of the benefits of being an investor in a resort instead of other asset classes is that you can enjoy your cash flow.

You can visit the property that you have invested in as a guest, enjoy great food and wine, and enjoy the property with your family. That is very tough to do with other investment niches.

The Pros Of Hospitality Investing

Through the Airbnb and VRBO business strategy, you can create cash flow through short-term rentals without owning a single property but controlling the property through a lease.

You can also systematize the entire process and outsource processes to virtual assistants.

Rehabbed resorts offer diverse revenue streams. Its symbiotic and complementary cash flow streams are any cash flow investor's dream.

Resorts provide a massive tax opportunity if eligible for the bonus depreciation.

Resort capital expenditures can often qualify for bonus depreciation, and the industry has a robust lending market. Often, the capital equipment can be secured with very attractive debt and receive full depreciation immediately. Importantly, these assets often lead to immediate revenue growth, which further accelerates the property's net operating income, which increases the value of the property.

Resort investments allow you to enjoy your cash flow without disrupting the profitability of the investment.

The Cons Of Hospitality Investing

In starting your own short-term rental business, you must treat it as a business. There is no shortcut to success, no get rich quick scheme, and no wealth without risk. The recipe for success is the same, you need the right mindset and strategy and must work very hard to build anything.

Hotels, their rooms, and their amenities need updating, daily cleaning, and restocking. This means that you will need to spend a significant amount of money on products and aesthetics.

While you may choose the quality over quantity approach, it doesn't matter which, as long as your guests are happy and the brand is invested in their happiness, too.

To survive as a hospitality investor, you need to keep guests happy and meet their needs. The same goes for the management. Knowing your team is the best way to increase the likelihood of a good reputation and subsequent profits. While investors won't be to blame for bad reviews, investing with a company that has a shaky reputation could mean that the whole project could be doomed if mismanaged.

With rehabbed resorts, seasonality is a huge risk. If the resort is in a coastal area, you need a strategy to get people to the resort in the winter. The same goes for ski resorts; you need a strategy to get people in the summer.

The economy is always a risk that can be managed through booking weddings out into the future and taking large deposits upfront. This way, if a recession hits, you can negotiate concessions in the contract but still have guests coming to your property for a wedding.

Niche #5: Mobile Home Parks

Across all media, mobile home park investing is beginning to be recognized as an attractive real estate sector.

When I researched this asset class years ago, people would look at me like I was crazy. So, what has made mobile home parks suddenly appear on the radar of investors?

The sector has always done extremely well, but investors are finally getting over the stigma. They are learning to appreciate the affordable housing that mobile home parks provide and the great returns for investors in providing affordable housing.

When investing in a mobile home park, you are essentially buying the land zoned to be rented out as separate lots to mobile home owners for a monthly or yearly fee.

The investors own the land, and most of the time, the residents own the mobile homes. Residents then pay rent for their lots.

The lots, and not the mobile homes, belong to park owners. Therefore, investing in mobile home parks has a lower cost per unit than any other type of real estate. Park owners can own more units for the same investment, spreading the risk and making the cash flow more consistent.

It is better to invest in mobile home parks where the residents own their homes. It provides a sense of ownership, which in turn provides a desirable community.

Mobile home parks where the parks own the homes and rent out the mobile homes have a different resident base.

So why are world-class investors Sam Zell and Warren Buffet invested in this niche?

Why have so many institutional and hedge fund investors entered the mobile home park niche? There is a massive demand for affordable housing in the United States.

The largest increase in poverty in the United States was recorded in 2020.[12] The Hamilton project conducted a study and found that 15% of households in the United States earn between

$1–$20,000 per year. It also found that 40% of households earn between $20,000–$40,000. The report shared that nearly half of households in the United States live below 250% of the federal poverty level.[13]

In the United States, over 70 million Baby Boomers are retiring. Over 10,000 Baby Boomers retire daily, with the average retirement savings balance of a Baby Boomer at less than $100,000 and the average Social Security benefit at $1,461.[14]

There is an affordable housing crisis, and it's getting bigger with a looming retirement crisis.

According to most economists, the demand for affordable housing literally grows daily, and this will continue for over a decade.

Along with soaring demand, there is a limited and dwindling supply. There are approximately 50,000 mobile home parks across the United States. Existing mobile home parks are shutting at a rate of 1% each year. Restrictive zoning laws make it nearly impossible to build a new park anywhere in the country.

---

[12] https://www.forbes.com/sites/tommybeer/2020/12/16/largest-increase-in-us-poverty-recorded-in- 2020/?sh=771dd48a32bd

[13] https://www.brookings.edu/research/a-dozen-facts-about-americas-struggling-lower-middle-class/

[14] https://www.forbes.com/sites/forbesfinancecouncil/2019/09/03/retirement-trends-of-baby-boomers/?sh=407d26b87378

This means that the supply of mobile home parks is decreasing, which increases the value of existing parks.

When you have soaring demand and decreasing supply, you have a massive opportunity.

The Pros Of Mobile Home Parks

It is a recession-proof asset class.

If you believe that the United States economy will continue to decline in the years ahead, under the weight of social programs and the drag of an aging population, mobile home parks are virtually the only form of real estate that performs better in a recession.

As America gets poorer, mobile home parks are the only form of housing devoted to this demographic.

It's very expensive for tenants to move, which means a lower tenant turnover rate than a traditional rental property. Another interesting barrier is the difficulty tenants have in moving their homes out of a mobile home park.

It costs around $5,000 to move a mobile home, so few tenants can ever afford to move. As a result, the revenues of mobile home parks are unbelievably stable. But what happens when a tenant cannot afford to continue to pay their rent? They usually have to abandon the home, and the park owner ends up with the title under abandoned property laws.

Investors must never lose sight of the fact that living in a mobile home park is rarely a resident's first choice. For many mobile home park residents, it's one step removed from living in their car or on the street.

You can raise the rent. However, the knowledge that you can increase rent whenever you like should always be balanced by knowing that your residents are held captive by their financial situation.

It is easier to raise the rent because residents have ownership of their homes. This provides a sense of ownership pride and makes it easier to change the rent to hedge against inflation.

Mobile home parks have some of the highest yields in commercial real estate.

There are fewer buyers for mobile home parks than other real estate niches. So, the supply/demand formula has always given mobile home parks a higher going-in rate of return.

Most parks have poor management and many opportunities to increase the net operating income, which increases returns for investors.

The Cons Of Mobile Home Parks

It's not a sexy investment, and it still has a stigma about it.

Some counties even try to stop operations (poorly operated parks, criminal activity), and most people don't want to live in one. These parks are where many people end up because they are entirely out of options.

You have lower credit-quality residents to pay rent for their lots. It is challenging to get most tenants to comply with maintenance responsibilities (keeping their lots well maintained).

Mobile home parks have less appreciation potential unless forced through operations and value add strategies.

Most banks struggle to understand mobile home parks, which makes it tougher to finance. In fact, you'll be hard-pressed to find a traditional bank or credit union that will give you a mortgage.

Large private equity funds are entering the space, which drives the prices up.

Niche #6: Self-storage Facilities

Self-storage property investments generate incredible returns for owners and investors.

10.6% of U.S. households rent self-storage units.[15] There are approximately 49,233 self-storage facilities. Investing in self-storage only really became popular in the mid-to-late 90s. Despite this, there are now almost as many self-storage facilities as all the Starbucks, McDonald's, and Subways combined.

There are great self-storage business opportunities in areas where the population is growing. Other signs that there may be opportunities for self-storage facilities are many local developments, businesses moving to the area, and business diversity. If there aren't many established self-storage properties or the area has minimally restrictive zoning, it may be the perfect investment opportunity.

Current properties should have great visibility, be close to the customer base, and have strong occupancy data.

There are plenty of value-add opportunities available for self-storage investments.

Independent owners control almost 80% of the self-storage properties in the U.S. Many of these "mom and pop" owners do not maximize their property's income potential.

You can increase income through merchandise sales, frequent rental increases, partnerships with local businesses, online marketing, and

---

[15] https://www.selfstorage.org/LinkClick.aspx?fileticket=fJYAow6_AU0%3d&portalid=0

relationships with moving companies. All these components can create tremendous value add opportunities with little capital investment.

Hunter Thompson shared that when an operator takes over a property, they can capitalize on monthly lease renewals to increase the rents immediately due to the "sticky" nature of the tenant base. This is especially beneficial if a property has been significantly below market rent before purchase.

According to Thompson, the most lucrative example of these low-risk value add components is to purchase facilities that are not currently offering U-Haul rentals. You then implementing this value add when the operator takes over a property. For example, a new operator can negotiate with U-Haul to have 10–15 U-Haul trucks on the property at little cost to the owner. Once the trucks are parked there, the property manager can rent the trucks out to tenants and receive a U- Haul commission for facilitating the transaction.

Other revenue-increasing strategies include retail (selling boxes and moving supplies) and stern management strategies (late fees, administration fees).

People are most likely to use self-storage during a life changing event, many of which require a moving truck.

Another strategy is purchasing properties based on in-place income that are not mandating their tenants' purchase insurance. Then, you implement this requirement immediately upon taking ownership of the property. Tenant insurance, essentially the same as insurance for a rented home or apartment, insures the items stored in the facility against losses due to flood, fire, theft, vandalism, etc.

Most top operators have relationships with self-storage-focused insurance companies who offer self-storage-specific insurance policies.

The Pros Of Self-storage Facilities

This asset class produces great cash flow for investors.

When the economy is good, people buy stuff. They need a place to store it. When the economy is in a recession, and people are moving, downsizing, or losing their house to a foreclosure or eviction, they need a place to store their belongings.

Americans have a culture of consumption and buying stuff. Estimates are that a third of storage space is filled with items that have been there for over three years.

Self-storage tenants are usually not price-sensitive. The self-storage rental fee is a small portion of a tenant's monthly disposable income. Operators can raise rents as demand increase without a massive impact.

Very few tenants will go through the trouble of renting a rental truck, packing up their stuff, and moving to another self-storage facility over a small rental increase. For investors, this can result in high cash-on-cash returns, especially when implemented over the long term.

Tenants also do not communicate regularly, allowing operators to raise rents selectively and increase the net operating income every year, which drives the property's value.

Self-storage is the only real estate asset class for which the Small Business Administration (SBA) will offer loans. There are some trade-offs with SBA loans, so it's advisable to look at all financing options before deciding which is best.

Tax benefits of depreciation. Like other real estate, self-storage benefits from the tax benefits of depreciation, which includes the loss in value of a building over time to wear and tear, deterioration and age. Depreciation is applied to the building, not the land.

The self-storage market is very fragmented, and properties remain in the hands of small, independent investors.

Institutional investors have started to come into the space through Real Estate Investment Trusts (REITs). The top six public companies control approximately 20% of the facilities, with approximately 80% of the facilities still controlled by independent owners.

Your tenants are boxes, so management is relatively smooth, and evictions are not hard, as you just have to get rid of the stuff. Tenants have rights, though, and you need to follow proper procedures.

The Cons Of Self-storage Facilities

Competition is fierce, since they are cheap to build since you need minimal infrastructure, and there is a demand for them.

The location and market positioning are key for the self-storage facility. You need to be in an area where there are people that need to store their excess stuff. You need people and businesses moving into the area. You need to be in an area that increases your visibility.

Hiring the right manager and staff is crucial to the performance of the investment. Since there is a high turnover of tenants when you offer month-to-month contracts, it requires active management to reduce vacancies.

Generally, the net operating income of a self-storage facility is lower than, for example, a multifamily property. The ratio of income generated versus expenses incurred is much higher, though.

Niche #7: Parking Garages

Most of us have parked our automobiles in a parking garage in a large city, town, or airport.

Parking garages are simple: you grab a ticket from the machine at a gate, park your car, and leave your car at the garage. When you return from whatever you were doing in the area, you pay for your parking at an automated machine and use your ticket to exit the garage.

It's a pretty simple user experience and business, and it is a great cash flow investment.

Parking garages are a misunderstood investment, which provides great opportunities for investors.

The parking garage niche is fragmented and has many favorable characteristics because of the high barriers to entry, consistent and predictable cash flows, and low recurring capital requirements.

Parking lots also avoid many of the potentially catastrophic issues plaguing multifamily properties, office buildings, and other tenant-orientated models face. These include nonpaying tenants, large upfront costs for fashionable improvements and businesses and agents imposing countless fees and commissions that can add up.

Parking garages also lack tenants demanding free rent, large up-front tenant improvements, and other concessions, or leasing agents looking for bonus commissions.

Many operators use centralized systems to control their garages and pay-on-foot and credit card technology to keep their costs down.

It is very technology-friendly with low overheads. You can literally have one person on-site managing a huge parking garage.

A favorable trend for parking garages is that parking in most cities and towns is becoming increasingly limited while demand is growing.

Parking will always be in demand, especially in highly populated cities and heavy transit areas.

There are more than 40,000 garages and surface parking lots in the US[16], with more than 105 million parking spaces and five million parking meters. The overall parking industry has generated about $29 billion in revenue and has more than 140,000 employees.

A limited supply with a growing demand positions investors favorably in this niche.

We will still need parking spaces and garages with trends like the sharing economy (Uber, Lyft), electric vehicles and even driverless vehicles.

Several disruptive companies in the space are currently looking to integrate the "connected car" technologies with "smart parking" technologies to make parking even more user-friendly.

This is why institutional investors are looking to invest $200–$250 million over the next three to five years.[17]

The $100 billion industry is poised for growth, with institutional investors and entrepreneurs capitalizing on opportunities in this niche.

---

[16] https://www.parkingtoday.com/articledetails.php?id=1600&t=the-future-of-the-100-billion-parking-industry

[17] https://www.parkingtoday.com/articledetails.php?id=1600&t=the-future-of-the-100-billion-parking-industry

The Pros Of Parking Garages

Parking garages reduce volatility and provide stable and consistent income, along with high cash yields and long-term revenue growth potential.

Parking garages have low-recurring capital requirements compared to traditional real estate assets. They have reduced income volatility through market cycles (people need parking no matter the economy).

Parking garages also provide the capability for immediate adjustments to market conditions and to hedge against inflation. Rates can be adjusted daily or even hourly. There are no long-term leases in most parking garages.

There is a high barrier to entry, and the existing supply is being replaced by new developments, especially with surface lots in urban areas. So not only is there a demand without a lot of supply, but the supply is actually shrinking.

Parking garages are not an actively sourced asset class. There are not a lot of existing parking garage deals for investors to buy. Investors might have to build garages instead of buying them.

The Cons Of Parking Garages

We live in a very fast-changing world. Because of technology and shifting consumer preferences, experts forecast that car ownership will decline.

Other threats to parking garages are competition from ride-sharing companies and improving mass transportation like light rail. Then, there is the so-far unfulfilled promise of autonomous vehicles from almost all automobile manufacturers.

Each of these threats should be considered a possible disruptor for the parking garage industry. Some of these threats have already started to impact parking garages in major cities.

Ride-sharing companies like Uber and Lyft have changed the need for car ownership especially in big cities. Drivers pick up passengers on their way to their final destination.

Mass transit is a genuine threat to parking garages. Most large cities implement strategic plans to improve regional connectivity to reduce traffic congestion and promote environmental stewardship. This has resulted in many metropolitan areas improving access to suburbs and nearby residential hubs through transportation other than cars.

Within five years, many automotive manufacturers expect to be producing driverless vehicles capable of parking themselves in "urban edge" locations, reducing the need for centrally located parking garages in cities.

Niche #8: Cell Tower Investments

We have all driven past cell towers and know exactly when we are not near one because of our poor cell phone reception.

Our phones have become super computers, and there's a lot of conversation about the very negative effects of 5G cell phone networks. We are very much aware of cell phone towers. It is a great niche with which to generate cash flow.

Cell tower investments offer investors exposure to the development, build-out, and construction of communication towers. The ultimate goal to lease the towers to multiple wireless service providers (AT&T, Verizon, T-Mobile) under long-term lease contracts for cash flow.

There are two business models when it comes to cell tower investments.

In the first model, the investor, or group of investors, owns the actual tower itself. This is the most lucrative.

You can build a tower for $100,000–$200,000. Major carrier lease rates can be $2,000–$6,000 per month, and you can have many carriers on your tower. However, you are limited to the carriers that operate in your market. Most markets in the United States have 4 to 5 carriers.

However, just because they are in your market, it does not mean that a specific location will work for them. There are many single carrier towers and quite a few that are zero carrier towers as well. Investors should not build a tower without a commitment from a tenant.

Operators can build and develop the cell phone tower, set up leases with several tenants, and then sell the investment to another investor.

The second business model is to own the ground/building with a tower/cell site and collect the lease revenue.

Carriers and tower companies will approach you if you have a good location. Unless you are in the business, it's challenging to seek out a carrier or tower company to build on your property.

It can be very profitable if you are lucky enough to get that call, sign a lease, and build the tower. You can also sell your lease via an easement to buyers with a lump sum payout.

The Pros Of Cell Tower Investments

There is a massive demand for cell tower investments since there has been tremendous growth in the use of cell phones in recent years, and this trend will continue.

We need more cell towers and other wireless infrastructure for our phones and mobile devices to work everywhere we go.

Smart phones have replaced radios, televisions, and computers as our preferred devices to connect to the world.

With 5G coming, demand is soaring for cell towers.

A former regional president of Verizon believes the United States will need 25 times the amount of existing wireless infrastructure in the next 10 years for 5G to work correctly.

4G technology connected everyone, and 5G technology will connect everything. 5G technology is the technology that will power the internet of things in the 4th industrial revolution.

Cell tower investments have very high caliber tenants, including blue-chip companies (AT&T, Verizon, T-Mobile). Therefore, leases are paid by very credit-worthy tenants.

Triple net leases are also very common, with the tenants paying all the cell tower expenses, taxes and maintenance.

It's a recurring revenue stream without the headaches of many real estate investments. The operating cost is also very low, and very little working capital is required.

Another very favorable factor for cell towers is the very low turnover rate in the industry. The industry average is less than 1% per year.

There are also high barriers to entry since no one wants the cell towers in their backyard.

Regardless of price changes due to inflation, cell towers are considered an asset expected to either maintain or increase in value over time for investors.

The Cons Of Cell Tower Investments

The risks in cell tower investments are carrier consolidation, demand for wireless broadband services, and slowing capacity. Also, wireless technology innovation could lead to less reliance on towers.

The financial performance of cell tower investments is tied to the ability of carriers to pay their leases. You can diversify your risk by having contracts with multiple carriers.

The niche also has a lot of competition for development and acquisition projects. It is a very red ocean for real estate entrepreneurs.

Cell tower investments are very illiquid investments, so your principal is tied up, but you do enjoy the cash flow from the investment.

Niche #9: Commercial Real Estate NNN Leases

One of my favorite commercial real estate cash flow strategies is triple net leases (NNN) on commercial retail properties.

Triple net lease investments are fantastic turnkey cash flow investments.

A triple net lease is a lease agreement on a property where the tenant agrees to pay all real estate taxes, building insurance, and maintenance (the three "nets"). In addition, the tenant pays any standard fees expected under the agreement (rent, utilities).

The triple net lease is considered a "turnkey" investment since the landlord is not responsible for operating expenses.

Commercial properties could include office buildings, shopping malls, industrial parks, or free- standing buildings operated by banks, pharmacies, or restaurant chains.

Tenants of triple net leases include Walgreens, CVS Pharmacy, McDonald's, Burger King, 7- Eleven, and International House of Pancakes.

Triple net lease properties can provide a reliable and predictable stream with low volatility and turnover. Few tenants that pay for everything, and the lease term is very long.

The typical lease term is 15 to 20 years, with built-in contractual rent escalation that hedges inflation. These leases also include lease renewal options for tenants.

The benefits for investors include long-term, stable income with the possibility of capital appreciation of the underlying property.

Investors can invest in high-quality real estate without concern for management operations, including vacancy factors, tenant improvement costs, or leasing fees.

When investors sell the underlying properties, they can roll their capital into another triple net lease investment without paying taxes through a 1031 tax-deferred exchange.

The Pros Of Commercial Real Estate NNN Leases

A triple net lease was designed to be landlord-favorable, protecting the landlord's interests against any changes, unexpected costs, and more.

It creates 100% pass-through charges so that ALL the burden, responsibilities, risks, and costs fall on the tenants. It was designed to help the landlord minimize their costs, responsibilities, and risks by shifting everything to tenants, maximizing the tenant's financial burden.

The turnkey nature allows you to not be geographically limited to your local market, and you can pick the best deal in the best location.

A triple net lease also makes the potential sale of a property more appealing to a potential buyer since you can sell a triple net lease property with the lease.

The Cons Of <u>Commercial Real Estate NNN Leases</u>

It is all about location, traffic count, population density, and demographics of a particular area for retail tenants. Keep in mind the level of research Starbucks, Target and Walmart conduct before opening a new location. Does the property have visibility, and is it near other retailers? Is it at store level, or is it part of an out-parcel? Is it easy to access?

Multiple factors determine if you have a good deal. Online businesses and e-commerce are disrupting many box-store categories. Avoid categories that online business and e-commerce could disrupt and properties with tenants that this threat could disrupt.

With most triple net lease properties, you have a few tenants and sometimes only one. If that tenant leaves, goes bankrupt or doesn't renew the lease, you will have no cash flow.

If you have only one commercial tenant, there is a risk of experiencing a complete vacancy.

It could be very hard to find another tenant that is a good fit for your location. It could significantly impact the property's value if you are trying to sell the property with a vacancy.

After a tenant has occupied the property for 10–25 years, the building may no longer be suitable to a new tenant when they leave. It becomes the property owner's responsibility to prepare the property, creating an attractive re-leasing process. It can create high capital expenditures after a lease period.

The financial strength of the entity that guarantees the lease is very important. A corporate and institutional entity or the franchisee could guarantee the lease. A corporate and institutional entity is more desirable.

Niche #10: Assisted Living And Memory Care Facilities

There is a massive demographic shift happening right now all over the world. Gene Guarino refers to it as the "Grey Tsunami."

According to Forbes, by 2040, the global population of those 65 years old and older will be 1.3 billion, double what it is today. In the United States, those 65 and older will hit 25% of the population by 2060.[18]

A massive wave of people from the baby boomer generation will become senior citizens in the next 20 years. In general, people live longer. Also, the children of aging seniors all work, and half of them are divorced. This means they are unable to take care of parents and grandparents, as previous generations could.

There is a massive demand for care businesses and housing for seniors and an insufficient supply to support this demand.

Entrepreneurs and investors have an enormous opportunity to address a vast senior housing and senior care challenge.

Besides the wave of this growing and accelerating global trend, senior housing is also a recession-resistant investment class. Assisted living communities continued to experience positive rent growth when all other sectors of commercial real estate declined during the 2007–2009 recession.

There are five categories of senior housing: Independent Living, Assisted Living, Memory Care, Skilled Nursing Facilities, and Hospice and Palliative care.

---

[18] https://www.forbes.com/sites/nextavenue/2016/05/09/how-to-make-money-from-the-global-aging- megatrend/?sh=77ec5d395a41

Independent living is facilities where seniors can enjoy independent living without assistance to manage their daily lives.

Assisted living communities serve residents with a wide range of health needs. They are regulated and licensed by each state to provide in-house support and services.

Memory care communities provide the same types of care as assisted living facilities but provide extra support for those that deal with dementia, memory loss, or the related disease of Alzheimer's.

Skilled Nursing Facilities are the most medically intensive senior housing segment, providing for those who need daily medical care.

Hospice and palliative care provide end-of-life care for people who are terminally ill.

Within these categories, you will find the following business models:

Continuous-care retirement communities are the age-in-one-place option for seniors. They have access to several residence rooms in one facility that provides assisted living services (25% on average) and memory care services (15% on average).

This way, residents can move into a facility independently and move around as they require more services. This age-in-place, continuous care model is well established.

The next model is an independent, assisted, and memory care living facility. These facilities have 50 to 300 beds built on several floors and look and feel like a hotel with rooms like mini-suites, with kitchens and private baths.

The facility has great amenities like dining rooms and community rooms to play Bingo, and more.

It is great for independent seniors who are looking for a community and want the option to secure additional care services they might someday need.

There are three levels of care needs: independent, assisted, and memory care.

Residential assisted living senior care homes are upscale, private pay, small group home environments. These are quickly becoming one of the most desirable homes for elderly persons needing 24/7 care.

One can find these residential assisted living homes in residential neighborhoods, or a cluster of homes built in a community. These homes provide a private room and bath in a small community of 8–16 people.

This model provides for a caregiver with a caregiver ratio of 5 to 1. The caregiver assists residents with cleaning, cooking, medication management, and personal needs, including toileting and bathing.

Cluster home senior care developments are a model that combines the continuous care model with residential assisted living senior care homes. A good example is 4 to 12 assisted living homes, two 12-bed memory care homes, and multiple independent living townhomes, villas, and cottages.

The 1980s TV show *Golden Girls* popularized the shared common space within independent living apartments/townhomes/villas/cottages model. Residents have a private bedroom and bath, with a shared common space. They pay a one-fee living arrangement that covers all expenses, including taxes and utilities.

Other options are social and cultural shared homes that are communities specifically for those that organize themselves by race, religion, or other social categories.

Home health care is also an option for seniors, including caregivers visiting the senior's residence to provide daily care. There are private pay options, or there is a government- subsidized option.

The government-subsidized/public pay is not the ideal model for investors since it relies on insolvent programs such as Medicare, Medicaid, and Social Security.

There are enormous opportunities in residential and commercial assisted living and memory care.

In this niche, there are two business models. You can own the real estate business and the care business. Or, you can choose to either own the real estate or own the care business.

You can invest as an active or passive investor in either business model.

The Pros Of Assisted Living and Memory Care Facilities

Senior living and, more specifically, residential and commercial assisted living and memory care facilities that rely on private pay are recession-proof investments. They do not depend on insolvent public institutions like Medicaid, Medicare, and other public programs.

It is an investment positioned to capitalize on one of the biggest trends in our lifetime, the aging global population. There is a massive demand and not enough supply.

The turnover rate is very low since the facility offers everything the tenants need. Because of the demand, there are, in many cases, waiting lists.

The cash flow and returns on the investments as an active or passive investor from the real estate or care business (or both) is incredible.

The Cons Of Assisted Living and Memory Care Facilities

Challenges include development and operating costs for active entrepreneurs in this space, construction activity, acquisition competition, economic changes, and regulation changes that could affect the market in the future.

The increasing costs of medical professionals and caregivers could eat away profit in these operations.

Some residential and commercial assisted living and memory care facilities didn't handle and manage the Covid-19 pandemic particularly well. Many families would in the future rather take care of mom and dad and look at hiring in-home care medical professionals to assist them with it.

In an economic environment where more and more people become poorer, the market size that can afford to live in residential and also commercial assisted living and memory care facilities without relying on government financial support, is shrinking.

Niche #11: Land Investing

The wealthiest people on the planet have owned and operated raw land for centuries.

Today, raw land presents another excellent opportunity for investors through creative strategies to generate cash flow.

With the right strategy, systems, and processes to implement the systems, this could be one of the best kept secret cash flow investing strategies out there.

One of the most creative strategies with raw land includes buying raw land for a fraction of the value and then selling the raw land slightly under market value for cash. Alternatively, the seller can finance buyers, where the seller acts as the bank.

This produces cash flow through the flipping system and payments received on the note from the land buyer.

Investors and entrepreneurs are only limited to their own imagination when it comes to raw land.

Investors can divide a single plot into several plots to increase its value and sell off the sub- divided plots. They can also develop on raw land to increase its use and value. Or, they can simply buy and hold raw land, as it has historically appreciated more often than not. Investors can lease or sell the land, long or short-term, collect rent or payments in full, or even finance payments through seller-financed structured sales.

You can implement this strategy with your computer and an internet connection. The entire system and processes can be automated through technology and software.

Raw land is very attractive as a cash flow source. It's easy to acquire, has little to no competition, and is low-cost to own and maintain.

Additionally, there is high potential for a quick profit, the flexibility to build or hold, and the potential for passive income.

The Pros Of Land Investing

Vacant, raw land is a very stable and abundant asset. However, there is a finite supply that can never increase.

Statistically, vacant raw-land-owners are very motivated to sell, and there is not much competition to buy the land.

It does not require a lot of money to get started in this niche. For as little as one or two thousand dollars, you can begin your raw land investments.

It is very inexpensive to own. When you buy a piece of land for the right price, there are no mortgage payments, no utility bills, nominal property insurance cost (if you have it at all), and extremely cheap property taxes. Raw and vacant land is a long-term, tangible asset that doesn't wear out, doesn't depreciate, and can't be broken, stolen, or destroyed.

Once you buy vacant raw land, you do not have to do anything with it physically. There is no dealing with tenants, toilets, bugs, mold, lawn care, leaking roofs, bursting pipes, broken furnaces, or the hundreds of other issues with owning buildings.

Raw land strategies can be systematized and automated to be quite simple and flexible. If done correctly, you can do everything, from due diligence to buying and selling remotely with a computer, internet connection, and a smartphone.

You do not have to visit the properties in person or do due diligence in person.

Raw land can be considered lower risk as it has fewer restrictions and codes than houses or buildings. It is very hard to steal raw land, and there is not much competition in the niche.

The raw land strategy does not involve bank financing, so easily borrowed money will not overinflate raw land prices and create a bubble.

When you act as the bank and collect payments on a note from the buyer, you can take back the raw land in case of a default and sell it again.

The profit and returns on raw land strategies are very attractive.

Selling land on owner financing terms can bring you monthly payments for 5 to 15 years on a single property.

This type of investing is very scalable.

The Cons Of Land Investing

It is very hard to find traditional financing for raw, vacant land. So, you cannot access the equity through collateralization strategies like a home equity line of credit (HELOC).

It is a very illiquid asset.

It also has fewer tax advantages. Although you can still depreciate certain improvements, such as roads or a new sewer system, vacant land leaves you without any structures to depreciate.

It does not generate cash flow right away after you purchase it. You would have to flip it for cash or structure a seller-financed deal to generate income from the asset.

Buyers of raw vacant land can be limited to zoning (i.e., residential, commercial, etc.) and permits. This can determine what you are able to do with the property.

Besides township restrictions and issues with the property itself, market conditions can partially dictate the success of your deal.

There can be physical issues with the property itself that could provide challenges.

Successful investors in this space avoid flat lots due to water runoff issues. They also avoid mountain properties and steeply graded land, which is harder to build on.

It is very important to have all the information on septic, sewer, water, and road access.

Like with any investment, you need to understand the asset class and the specific market in which you are buying. You also need to be clear on your goals, strategies, risk management strategies, and exit strategy.

Niche #12: Agriculture Investing

Commodities are a very attractive asset class in inflationary times, and agriculture is an excellent commodity for many reasons.

Investing in agriculture has become very attractive. It is not correlated to the stock market, and it provides one of the basic human needs, food.

The supply of food is not keeping up with demand. Not even close.

There is a rapid growth of the global population, a shrinking supply of arable farmland, and an increased demand from developing economies such as China, Russia, and India.

An article in the *Economist* states, "In the next 40 years, humans will need to produce more food than they did in the previous 10,000 years put together. But with sprawling cities gobbling up arable land, agricultural productivity gains decreasing, and demand for biofuels increasing, supply is not keeping up with demand."[19]

The Guardian paper shared, "The world has lost a third of its arable land due to erosion or pollution in the past 40 years, with potentially disastrous consequences as global demand for food soars, scientists have warned."[20]

The supply of arable farmland is shrinking, and due to many factors, the demand for food and agricultural products is increasing.

The human population has skyrocketed over the last couple of centuries.

---

[19] https://www.economist.com/finance-and-economics/2014/12/30/barbarians-at-the-farm-gate
[20] https://www.theguardian.com/environment/2015/dec/02/arable-land-soil-food-security-shortage

According to the Food and Agriculture Organization of the United Nations, the world population will reach 9.7 billion by 2050.

In a report titled *World Agriculture: Towards 2015/2030*, the FAO concludes that there will be a higher demand for food, and agriculture production will have to increase by 70% by 2050 to meet demand.[21]

There is a shrinking supply of labor in the agricultural sector.

Jim Rogers, famous commodities investor, and author, remarked, "The average age of an American farmer is 58, and the average age in Japan is 68." Not enough people are going into the farming business, and it is lowering the supply of labor.

Demand for agricultural products is growing, fueled by population growth and income growth in developing nations. The supply of farmland and supply of labor to work the land is shrinking.

Technology will increase efficiency and fill the void for the lack of available labor to work the land. Still, the massive demand and limited supply provides an enormous opportunity in the agriculture sector.

Agriculture is a demand-driven, non-correlated asset that is less volatile.

There are ways to position yourself as an investor in this niche and capitalize on its opportunities. You don't need to become a commercial farmer. You also don't need to buy stocks and exchange-traded funds in the stock market blindly.

You can directly invest in agriculture as a passive investor. Examples are agriculture syndications that feature sustainable or organic production methods, including cannabis, timber, teak, coffee, row crops, livestock and indoor agriculture.

The legal cannabis business has taken the United States and the world by storm. With the popularity of cannabidiol (CBD) products, medicinal

---

21 http://www.fao.org/3/y4252e/y4252e.pdf

applications, and recreational use, the cannabis market is currently estimated at $22.9 billion.[22]

The size of just the medicinal cannabis market is estimated to be $14.46 billion.[23]

Cannabis becomes legalized in more countries, states and provinces around the world. Medicinal applications, cannabidiol (CBD) products, and recreational use continue to grow at a staggering pace. This provides an incredible opportunity for investors to invest in businesses, farming businesses and even invest directly in individually allocated and professionally managed farm parcels.

You can, as an accredited investor, participate by directly investing in these opportunities. The wealthiest families have invested in timber for centuries.

John Malone, the former CEO of Tele-Communications Inc. and one of America's wealthiest individuals, owns 2.2 million acres of timber. Another extremely prominent and wealthy American media mogul, Ted Turner, owns over 2 million acres of timber. Additionally, the Harvard Endowment Fund[24], worth $41.9 billion, holds approximately 10% of its assets in timber investments.

The teak tree is a tropical hardwood that has been used for high-end construction, furniture, and luxury items for centuries. Because of the remarkable and unique qualities of teak, including resistance to fire, rot, termites, and disease, teak is an obvious choice when building a product that will last.

As a result of the longevity and beautiful golden color, teak prices are high and consistently increase each year. One of the best reasons to own teak is the long cycle cash flow it provides.

---

[22] https://www.mordorintelligence.com/industry-reports/cannabis-market

[23] https://www.emergenresearch.com/industry-report/medical-cannabis-market

[24] https://www.harvard.edu/about-harvard/endowment/

Long cycle investments protect against short-term fluctuations in the markets and provide a long- term basis of stability to wealth. Short-term cash flow is current and may vary widely over the years.

It provides great stability to an overall portfolio for this very reason.

Trees literally grow through extended periods of economic recession. They continue compounding in value, annually adding to their worth no matter what the markets are doing.

Forestry, and specifically teak, in this case, produces harvests on a 25-year or longer cycle. This provides lump-sum distributions of return periodically. You can use those funds to pay for education, start businesses, or contribute back to the corpus of the trust or family foundation.

You do not need to be a billionaire, an endowment for a family office to invest in timber and teak.

You can invest passively in timber and teak farms that allow individual owners to own their very own parcel and provide physical ownership of an agricultural hard asset. This combines land and production of a commodity that is in historically high demand.

Coffee is a proven product consumed globally by billions of people with sustainable and growing demand and limited and declining supply worldwide.

Fun fact: coffee is a $90 billion industry annually, second only to oil in terms of dollar volume traded!

Cacao is the primary ingredient for chocolate. According to research, the global chocolate market was valued at around USD 103.28 billion in 2017.

The global demand for coffee and chocolate is massive. The best area in the market to compete is in on the high end through specialty coffee and chocolate.

Another great way to invest directly in agriculture is through coffee and cacao land parcels in Panama and Belize.

You can passively invest in specialty coffee and cacao farms in Belize and Panama. You invest in parcels that are professionally managed with experienced turnkey management in place. The planting, farming, harvesting, processing, marketing and coffee sales are all done for investors.

The operating company controls the entire process. They successfully harvest, process, and sell the crops as part of their turnkey operation.

In this investment, you own the land that is an appreciating real hard asset, deeded to you, safe and secure, private and offshore.

The strategy helps you diversify away from traditional real estate in your own backyard and into productive farmland in an uncorrelated international market.

These coffee and cacao parcels produce sustainable long-term cash flow.

Returns start slow, while Mother Nature takes her course and increases year after year, becoming increasingly powerful with time.

You can also directly invest in row crops, livestock, and indoor agriculture.

Row crops are commodity crops such as wheat, corn, and soybeans and are staples of almost every country's diet.

Historically, investors used row crops as a hedge against inflation. In addition to being consumed, these products are often used in feed for livestock. They are the raw ingredients of almost everything we eat. The need for these crops will never subside; grains, corn, and soy are so prevalent in the food industry that demand is guaranteed to stand the test of time.

The United States is the largest grain exporter globally by quite a significant margin, and recent price stability is a good sign for both farmers and investors alike.

When you roll your cart up to the meat cooler at the grocery store, chances are you've seen a wide variety of beef. Aside from the different cuts, there are many labels explaining how the beef was produced. Even ground beef has a plethora of options to choose from: grass-fed, organic, naturally raised; and the list goes on. There are ways for investors to directly invest in each variety of livestock through syndications.

There are various ways to produce crops through indoor agriculture, including vertical farming, aquaponics, hydroponics, and aquaculture. Each production system has different qualities.

However, they all need indoor facilities to lower environmental impacts sometimes associated with traditional outdoor farming.

These indoor facilities can include greenhouses, storage containers, refurbished warehouses, and other building structures.

Institutional investors and the wealthy have long understood the value of private investments in agriculture.

You can now invest in a similar manner in this very attractive asset class.

"Agriculture is going to be the big thing in the next 20 years." – Jim Rogers

The Pros Of Agriculture Investing

World hunger and food security are two very pressing issues. There is an enormous demand for food, farmland, and farmers and not nearly enough supply. It will become a much bigger problem, providing a huge opportunity for entrepreneurs and investors in this niche.

Direct investing in agriculture provides portfolio diversification for investors outside of the stock market.

Investing in offshore agricultural investments also provides international diversification.

Investing as a passive investor allows you to participate directly in agriculture investments without becoming a farmer.

Direct agricultural investments provide great tax benefits for investors. Examples are depreciation (lots of equipment and tools to depreciate), favorable property taxes (each country and state is different but has incentives), and creative tax-advantaged strategies like land conservation easements.

It provides fantastic long-term cash flow and income, and returns increase and get stronger over time. Overall and long-term returns are very attractive.

Agriculture is a great inflation hedge.

The Cons Of Agriculture Investing

When you are investing in agriculture, you are partnering with Mother Nature. The success of your harvests and the quality of your crops depends on the weather and climate.

It also takes time and requires patience; this is not a space for people that want to make a quick buck. You have to grow crops and take care of them until harvest and then sell the crops.

You need to invest for the next 10, 20, or 30 years, and even for the next generation.

Niche #13: Energy Investments

Energy is the largest and most valuable market segment on earth, responsible for approximately 10% of the world's gross domestic product (GDP), placing it second only after health care.[25]

Energy generates more revenue than any other sector.

We need energy in every area of our lives to survive, so there is an enormous demand for all forms of energy. Nothing happens without electricity, oil, gas, coal, nuclear, biofuel and solar and wind energy resources.

Investing in the energy sector can be complex, since the industry spans from drilling for oil to renewable businesses, focusing on wind and solar power generation.

There are two excellent cash flow opportunities in this sector. Firstly, direct investing in oil and gas exploration. Secondly, investing directly in a business specializing in a process using distillation units to produce shale oil, industrial solvents, and non-condensable gas products using a proprietary process.

Oil makes the world go around, and there's no sign of that changing any time soon. Petroleum remains in high demand, as it is an efficient way to generate energy and it also has many uses in industry, as it can be used as a lubricant and is a key component in creating plastics.

Natural gas, for its part, is a popular energy source for heating and cooking. It can also be converted into diesel fuel and electricity and is essential in creating chemical fertilizers.

---

[25] https://www.enerdata.net/publications/executive-briefing/world-energy-expenditures.html

Broadly speaking, there are four kinds of oil and gas investments:

Exploration companies or projects buy or lease land and invest money in drilling. If they strike oil, the investment can pay off ten times over – sometimes much more if the company uses borrowed money to finance operations. If not, they may lose nearly everything they invested in that particular project. Pure exploration companies are best suited for those with a very high tolerance for investment risk. These plays are risky and highly speculative and you can lose your entire investment if you do not strike oil.

Developing projects drill near proven reserves, hoping to unlock further value. These are somewhat less risky and speculative, but there are never any guarantees that their efforts on any one plot of land will pay off.

Income projects involve acquiring plots of land, either through lease or purchase, above proven oil and gas reserves. These seek to create a steady stream of income over and above expenses. This is generally the safest way to get involved specifically in drilling and extraction operations, and is more of an income play.

The risk is that the oil or natural gas will run out faster than expected. This investment is for those seeking a passive income stream but who can take on more risk than those investing in other traditional income generators, like investment-grade bonds and annuities.

Services and support companies provide a nearly unlimited menu of supporting services to the oil and gas industry. Examples include transportation, shipping, and logistics companies, pipeline companies, construction and rigging companies, drilling and refining hardware and equipment manufacturers, refiners, and many others. Investing in these companies is similar to investing in any other company involved in business-to-business services, logistics, technology, and the like.

Some of these investments don't rely on increasing fuel prices to be profitable.

Direct investing as passive investor in oil and gas exploration is very lucrative from a cash flow perspective. It is tax-advantageous but has some risk associated with it.

Do not only be enticed by the attractive tax advantages. It's pointless to invest in anything to reduce taxes legally but losing your capital.

Another way is to invest directly in business that uses a proprietary process utilizing distillation units to produce shale oil, industrial solvents, and non-condensable gas products.

What if you could invest in an asset class that produces a highly sought-after commodity without many of the downside risks considered normal in the commodities markets?

And what if you could get the same tax treatment as when you invest in the oil and gas sector, where the depreciation/depletion offsets the tax liability on your ordinary income?

One of my favorite investments is a direct investment opportunity in the cleaner energy space.

Here, you invest in distillation units to produce shale oil products using a proprietary closed-loop process. This process derives high-demand liquid products and shale oil from coal.

The patented technology provides a reliable income stream through several products for use in the following industries: manufacturing steel and power plant coal boilers, cosmetics, dyes, resins, pharmaceuticals, transportation fuels, firefighting liquids, agricultural products, solvents, and oil field solvents.

The distillation units in the proprietary distillation process transform raw coal into a much cleaner, hotter-burning, and better finished product that lowers emissions and has higher energy efficiency.

This finished product helps power plants meet strict Environmental Protection Agency (EPA) standards, reduce toxic mercury emissions, and key sulfur emissions. The lighter weight of the product makes it easier to handle. The homogenized and dry fuel is easier to burn. The byproducts are also commercially viable products.

There is high demand for the product. Much of it being imported, so there is not nearly enough domestic supply. The operator has existing contracts with some internationally recognized companies.

In many cases, the costs for the physical commodity are locked in for 10 or 15 years, reducing another level of risk.

The investment in these distillation units, with a proprietary process to provide "cleaner energy," provides very strong cash flows and powerful tax incentives without the risk of exploratory oil and gas drilling.

The Pros Of Energy Investments

It provides portfolio diversification. When gas prices rise, economies tend to slow. This could cause the rest of your stocks and funds to stumble. But when oil and gas prices rise, oil and gas investments tend to rise with them. An exposure to oil and gas investments can help insulate your portfolio against economic slowdowns caused by oil shocks.

There is significant profit potential. Investments in smaller companies and limited partnerships can occasionally pay off big. A single well can generate many times its cost if drillers strike oil, and the well can pay dividends for many years.

There are some tax advantages to oil and gas investing. For instance, the Internal Revenue Service (IRS) allows companies to deduct for depletion, an allowance similar to depreciation in rental real estate. This is a way of accounting for the gradual exhaustion of mineral supplies in a given plot of land. Equipment can also be depreciated.

Energy investments are great inflation hedges.

The Cons Of Energy Investments

There is plenty of volatility in this asset class. Oil and gas investments can be subject to wild price swings, especially when investing in smaller companies. Getting involved in exploratory drilling projects can mean easily losing a great amount of money –all of it in some cases.

Diversification is the key to oil and gas investing. Losses of 50% or more are not unusual, and you can lose everything on any project.

Your investment is not liquid.

Geopolitical events of very unstable regions such as the middle east impact the energy sector directly. The volatility of the region produces volatility in the asset class. Wars, terrorism, and economic warfare are a constant in the world we live in and impact energy.

Politics impact the energy niche directly. A change in presidential administration can bring with it massive changes to the energy niche.

The massive trend towards greener and more sustainable energy sources and the emergence and growth of electric vehicles will impact certain energy sectors positively and certain energy sectors negatively.

Niche #14: Music Royalties

Music will rake in $41 billion by 2030, according to a recent report from Goldman Sachs[26] — over 80 percent of that from streaming sites like Spotify or Pandora. Every time a song is streamed online, somebody is getting paid royalties.

For example, when someone streams Eminem's "Lose Yourself," somebody's collecting what are known as performance royalties.

Eminem himself makes money. However, in the case of "Lose Yourself," another production company called FBT Productions is also cashing in since it owns rights to a substantial chunk of Eminem's song catalog.

There are hundreds of thousands of these rights holders out there that aren't necessarily the artists themselves.

Peter Thall, a music attorney, said musicians often have a hard time borrowing from a bank. Selling off performance royalty income to investors can help a musician raise money.

Artists looking to raise some quick cash can sell their future royalties. Investors can then get paid every time a certain song or portfolio of songs is played on the radio, streamed, or heard on TV.

Musicians can sell their royalty streams to fund a new album, tour, or other projects. They can also use it to fund their retirement income, buy a house or vehicle, fund a family emergency, support a side project

---

[26] https://www.billboard.com/articles/business/7949040/music-industry-will-hit-41-billion-by-2030-according-to- new-goldman-sachs

or charitable cause, diversify away from music as their sole source of income, fund investments of their own, and pay off debt.

So, what makes music royalties an interesting alternative investment opportunity?

Royalties offer a good degree of yield. If you buy at the right price, you can get yields far greater than what you can get from bonds or savings accounts, or other types of investments.

There are three reasons to invest in music royalties. Music royalties have consistency (quarterly payments). They have stability (older assets reach a "plateau level" of earnings you can generally rely on). Royalties' divergence from broader market returns is a good reason to invest.

What happens if the stock market crashes? That doesn't affect anything – you still get paid your royalties.

This uncorrelated asset class that's consistent, stable, and high yield is very attractive for investors.

The Pros Of Music Royalties

Music royalties can provide high income throughout the music's copyright period.

Global central banks also do not impact music royalties that subject investors and regular citizens to negative interest rates.

The value of the intellectual property can rise over time. You might remember what happened after the passing of Michael Jackson. His net worth surged after his death in 2009.

Billboard writes that MJ Inc., the firm that controls Jackson's branding, earned at least $1 billion since his passing. Roughly half of it, $494 million, is tied directly to music sales and royalties.

His royalties have increased by 70% since his passing.[27]

---

[27] https://www.billboard.com/articles/news/957679/how-michael-jackson-made-1-billion-since-his-death

There are other ways that music royalties can appreciate in value. Intellectual property in music typically increases in value when others demand to use, license or reproduce it over time.

The continuation of their income streams can be significant depending on the length of the copyright protection. Some copyrights will outlive many of the companies trading on the stock market today. Depending on the origin of the musical work, a copyright could last up to 70 years after the death of the artist, songwriter, or musician.

Intellectual property is an asset you can own for decades, providing returns based on the demand for its use long after its creation and passing of its creators.

Diversification from the stock market is one of the benefits of music royalty investment.

The Cons Of Music Royalties

Music depreciates quickly. After the first couple of years, royalties can drop by 75% or more and continue a steady decline. It is rare for music to continue producing strong income for 10, 20, 30 years or more. This makes the tail end of the copyright term potentially not worth much.

Collections of dozens of songs earn most of their income from a single song. Other auctions are for single-song royalty streams.

There typically are seller buyback options. Some auctions have a clause allowing the seller to buy back the property within one year. This gives the buyer a quick return on investment.

However, it ensures that if the property increased in value, the seller would snatch it back. These are not great terms.

There is a limited market to resell. How many people do you know who buy music royalties? It is a very small and niche market compared to, for example, the stock market.

There is a significant marketing risk. What if no one is selling the music? You don't have the right to make deals on the song when you purchase the royalty rights. You only have access to the income generated. For this reason, you want to look at owning only partial songs so that the artists and recording companies are retaining skin in the game to continue to sell the product.

One of the risks and benefits of music intellectual property is that a song's popularity can go in cycles. Think of 1960s music becoming popular in the 1980s and 1990s. Think of 1980s music becoming popular in the 2000s. Just as any asset has cycles, so does music.

Niche #15: Automated Machines Investing

Automated machines are an exciting investment niche that can be very profitable.

I identify two very profitable investments in this investment niche: vending machines and automated teller machines (ATMs).

Vending machines are great for active investors. For investors that are looking to invest more passively, ATMs provide a great opportunity.

There are plenty of vending machines in the United States, approximately 7 million of them.

$100 million Americans will use vending machines.

We all walk past a vending machine at some stage during our day. We find them at airports, schools, offices, malls, gyms and other public places.

What you can buy through a vending machine is only limited to the imagination of the vending machine's owner. When most people think of vending machines, they imagine the candy and toy machines located at the exits of supermarkets or the candy and soda machines found just about everywhere. These are, however, not the only options when it comes to vending machines.

Refrigerated vending machines provide snacks and lunch items. People can buy personal necessities in toiletry vending machines in public restrooms and even rent videos in vending machines. Airports have electronics vending machines that sell wireless headsets and chargers.

The vending machine niche is a great niche to generate cash flow for creative entrepreneurs.

There are three ways to get into the vending machine business. You can do it yourself, or you can buy an existing vending machine route. Alternatively, you can buy a franchise or business opportunity.

Everyone knows about ATMs (automated teller machines), and everyone hates to accept the high fees at ATMs.

What if you were the business collecting the fees on the other end of the transaction? What about the cashless society trend that seems to be accelerating?

Did you know that there are 45 million Americans who are unbanked or underbanked and do not have access to payment systems other than cash? That is approximately 30% of American households.

Cash is still the most frequent method of payment. People make one-third of all transactions with cash, and more than 50% of those transactions are under $25.00

PayPal CEO Dan Schulman told the New York Times, "I would never predict the death of cash over the next decade or two. I think cash is going to be with us for a long time to come."

Michael Vaughn, the CEO of Venmo, says, "It's still decades and decades. It's going to take our lifetime and our kids' lifetime before you start to see this work itself out (before cash dies)."

ATM portfolios continue to do well, and the use of cash continues to climb despite all the new technology in the marketplace.

One of the most common misconceptions around ATM investing is that due to new technology, cryptocurrency, Apple Pay, Google Wallet, and all, using cash is declining.

Fintech is disrupting the banking industry. Customers migrating to digital channels contribute to banks closing unprofitable, low-traffic branches.

Account-holders consider ATMs the number one self-service channel and interaction method with a bank. So, ATMs will fill the transactional gap created as banks continue to close.

Today, ATMs are mini-banks. They not only dispense cash, but allows users to open accounts, accept and deposit cash and checks, get loans and make payment. ATMs also offer cardless options with near field communication technology (NFC) also known as tap and pay, multi- currency dispensers, access to remote live tellers, the ability to remit money halfway around the world, and issue passbooks, prepaid cards, stamps, and more.

ATMs have transformed into a multi-dimensional interactive touchpoint for consumers requiring secure, reliable access to cash while also enabling an increasingly wide variety of transactions.

ATMs have reduced the costs for the service provider, the bank while increasing the convenience for the consumer.

This mindset change of banks will be a key ingredient for the rebirth of the ATM. Embracing the ATM's expanded role and integrating it with mobile and web banking creates a powerful service platform that forms an essential ingredient to customer loyalty and satisfaction.

"ATMs have become far more than machines that dispense cash. They are portals into a full array of technologies that let people bank anytime, anywhere. ATMs are now at the forefront of omnichannel technologies that are redefining the digital economy." – Bill Nuti, CEO, NCR.

You can invest directly in the strong ATM fundamentals and trends through ATM syndicated investments structured to produce strong cash flow.

It also offers phenomenal tax advantages as the equipment and ATMs themselves will depreciate every year.

The Pros Of Automated Machine Investing

One of the key attractions in buying a vending machine business is the low start-up cost. You can pay as little as $150 to $400 per machine plus inventory to get started. Franchise opportunities make it easy to buy.

If you are buying an existing vending machine business, your start-up costs could be higher than when buying a few machines as a new franchise. However, your purchase will come with established locations and a good understanding of existing cash flow.

ATMs provide strong, predictable cash flow in the double digits with very little volatility. It provides real asset ownership (machines) in a recession-resistant investment.

ATMs provide aggressive tax benefits.

ATMs help investors capitalize on the steady uptrend in the use of cash and ATM use over the last decade.

The Cons Of Automated Machine Investing

It takes time to get a vending machine business off the ground. When starting a franchise vending machine business, realize that it takes time to place machines in locations and generate revenues.

You must follow a strict restocking schedule with vending machines. Stocking the machines can get burdensome, especially if you have a lot of them. If you are unable to do this yourself, you must hire someone.

Vending machines are notoriously the targets of vandalism. It is imperative to find quality locations where machines are within sight of staff or in secure locations.

ATMs are constantly at risk of technology obsolescence.

With central bank digital currencies (CBDCs) on the horizon and with the global monetary and financial system in the process of undergoing a reset, physical cash could be history. ATMs could still feature in a post-cash world as most of them are mini banks and could replace bank branches. They offer the ability to automate all the services performed inside the bank currently by people.

Niche #16: Stock Market Cash Flow

Paper assets such as stocks, bonds, and notes provide investors liquidity, agility, and the ability to scale investments fairly quickly.

I am not "anti" the stock market. However, I am against passively buying and holding stocks in the stock market and entirely against any qualified retirement plans.

Average investors buy and hold stocks, bonds, and mutual funds in a portfolio or a qualified retirement plan.

Markets only do three things. They go up, they go down, and they go sideways.

Average investors only make money when the markets go up. Average investors bet on the 33% probability.

Professionals have strategies to create cash flow in the stock market whether markets go up, down, or sideways.

One of the strategies that professional investors use to generate cash flow in the stock market is the covered call income strategy.

Options strategies are beyond the scope of this book, and it is not my intention to share information on options and options trading. I will only cover a cash flow strategy for the stock market involving an options trade.

To explain cash flow strategy for the stock market cash flow, I will briefly explain two option strategies, call and put options.

The Options Guide[28] defines call options as "an option contract in which the holder (buyer) has the right (but not the obligation) to buy a specified

---

[28] https://www.theoptionsguide.com/

quantity of a security at a specified price (strike price) within a fixed period of time (until its expiration).

For the writer (seller) of a call option, the option represents an obligation to sell the underlying security at the strike price if the option is exercised. The call option writer is paid a premium for taking on the risk associated with the obligation."

The Options Guide defines put options as "an option contract in which the holder (buyer) has the right (but not the obligation) to sell a specified quantity of a security at a specified price (strike price) within a fixed period of time (until its expiration).

For the writer (seller) of a put option, the put option represents an obligation to buy the underlying security at the strike price if the option is exercised. The put option writer is paid a premium for taking on the risk associated with the obligation."

A covered call is a trade in which the seller of the call options owns the corresponding number of shares of the underlying stock.

A covered call sells this right to someone else to essentially rent the shares in exchange for cash, with the option to buy the stock that you own on or before the option contract's expiration date at a predetermined price called the strike price.

So essentially, you are renting the stock that you own with an option to buy to another trader and collecting a premium payment for doing so.

When you sell a covered call, you get paid in exchange for giving up a portion of future upside. Here is a bullish scenario/example:

January 1st   Buy 1000 shares of Hey Boet Company at $50.00 per share.

January 1st   Sell 1000 Hey Boet Company call options for $4.00 per share, expires on June 30th, exercisable at $55.00.

June 30th   Stock closes at $60.00 per share and the option is exercised because it is above $55.00 per share and you receive $55.00 per share for your shares.

July 1st   Your profit is $5.00 per share on your shares (you bought it for $50.00 per share and sold them at $55.00 per share) You also collected $4.00 of premium collected from the sale of the option. Your total profit is $9.00 per share and you had 1000 shares which provides a total profit of $9000.00 or 18%.

Let's assume you buy Hey Boet Company stock for $50.00 per share, believing it will rise to

$60.00 per share within one year.

You're also willing to sell at $55.00 within six months, giving up further upside while taking a short-term profit.

In this scenario, selling a covered call on the position might be an attractive strategy.

The stock's option chain indicates that selling a $55.00 six-month call option will cost the buyer $4 per share premium. You could sell that option against your shares, which you purchased at $50.00 and hope to sell at $60.00 within a year.

Writing this covered call creates an obligation to sell the shares at $55.00 within six months if the underlying price reaches that level.

You get to keep the $4 in premium plus the $55.00 from the share sale for the grand total of $59.00, or an 18% return over six months.

On the other hand, you'll incur a $10.00 loss on the original position if the stock falls to $40.00.

However, you get to keep the $4 premium from selling the call option, lowering the total loss from $10.00 to $6.00 per share.

If the share price stays between $50.00 to $54.00 per share and the option expires after six months, you keep the $4 of premium collected ($4000 total).

You can then repeat the strategy and collect more premiums.

The covered call strategy is a great strategy to collect stock market cash flow where the underlying stock shares go up and go sideways.

There is an additional trade strategy to protect your position when the price of the share goes down, but that is beyond the scope of this book.

Professional cash flow investors do not buy in the hope that the security or asset price goes up.

Professional cash flow investors buy securities and assets at a discount and generate cash flow from them. Then, they buy more until the asset value reaches the top of the asset cycle, during which they exit.

Trading covered calls will be an active investment strategy that you can do yourself with the help of a mentor or coach.

The Pros of Stock Market Cash Flow

Covered call option strategies to generate stock market cash flow are a great way to leverage the security you own to generate cash flow from your shares.

You collect the premium upfront, and it is yours to keep regardless of what happens next.

It reduces the overall cost of buying the shares since you can deduct the premiums paid against the cost of the shares.

If you are long a certain stock, meaning you are very bullish about the stock's growth potential, you can get paid to hold the stock.

If you sell covered calls monthly, you can increase the earnings from owning the shares 12 times. You can create monthly income from owning the shares.

A covered call strategy can help offset downside risk.

The Cons of Stock Market Cash Flow

If you sell covered calls against shares that you own that rise sharply in price, it can cap your profit potential.

Selling a covered call does not protect you from losses. It can reduce your loss on your position when the price goes down but does not protect your downside.

Call sellers have to hold onto underlying shares or contracts, or they'll be holding naked calls, which have theoretically unlimited loss potential if the underlying security rises.

In a market crash, you would have to buy your options back to sell your shares and minimize losses, increasing your overall cost.

The buyer of the call option could exercise the option when the option is "in the money," a term used when the share price is at or above the strike price. This means that you now had to sell the shares, and you no longer own the shares you are bullish on.

Remember, there is no risk-free way to invest in the stock market. There are no guarantees.

Niche #17: Mortgage Notes

Real estate mortgage notes are one of the most effective investment strategies in real estate. You get many of the benefits that go along with real estate investments without the management headaches.

Real estate notes include mortgages for primary and secondary homes (first and second mortgages), along with home equity lines of credit (HELOCs) and bridge loans.

People can act as banks by funding these lending instruments independently or participating in investment groups specializing in mortgage lending.

There are mortgage notes on every type of real estate, including: single-family homes, small multiunit homes, townhomes, apartment complexes, commercial strip malls, and industrial buildings. However, we categorize them as residential or commercial mortgage notes.

There are also different types of mortgage notes: secured, unsecured, private loans (hard money, seller financing), and institutional loans.

Performing notes are notes that are being paid and have not been delinquent. Nonperforming notes are notes that have defaulted.

Mortgage notes are a great way to diversify your portfolio while providing cash flow, minus the headaches of being a landlord.

Investing in a note is essentially putting up a lump sum to purchase a contract that promises to pay you a stream of payments. The investor can count on regularly receiving this monthly payment, regardless of what happens in the unreliable stock market.

When someone purchases a house, they make a down payment, usually 20–30%, in order to take the house's title. Then, they continue to make monthly mortgage payments to the bank with interest. If the homebuyer does not make payments, the bank will take the house back through the foreclosure process.

Sometimes, the bank needs cash quickly and will want to sell this stream of payments to an investor for a lump sum.

Mortgage notes are backed and collateralized by real estate. So, you really increase your chances of a profitable note when you buy it at a steep discount, relative to the value of the property and the number of repairs needed. This provides a high yield, and it is collateralized by a property that you would not mind taking ownership of if the note defaults.

You do not need to be as actively involved with mortgage notes as other real estate investments. There are no toilets that need to be fixed. JP Morgan Chase does not worry about broken toilets. They worry about the payments on the mortgage notes on their books.

Since you are dealing with paper, you can invest in notes in different markets, making it an easier to scale and grow. You can even scale your mortgage note portfolio faster than most traditional real estate portfolios.

Instead of spending your time on landlord and management headaches, you can spend it on finding deals, partners and investors for your note portfolio.

Mortgage notes are an opportunity for creativity. The only limit to your strategies is your imagination.

Due diligence is very important in mortgage notes and includes:
- the value of the property in its as-is condition;
- any liens or encumbrances on the property that might affect or jeopardize your position;
- any unpaid taxes, potential tax liens, or tax deed sales;

- the annual tax rate;
- whether the current lender possesses all required paperwork (the original note, mortgage, and other documents);
- the payment history on the note; and
- the borrower's credit score.

The Pros Of Mortgage Notes

Mortgage notes are truly passive income investments compared to other real estate investments.

You can manage a note portfolio (either performing or nonperforming) from the phone and computer without ever leaving the house or office. This enables servicers to manage notes on properties all across the nation.

A performing note is secured by real physical property, and there are multiple means of protecting a note investment. It involves little or moderate risk to own a secured lien tied to property, especially if the property has equity. A note owner has a right to foreclose on the property and to recoup some, or all, of the initial investment.

The investor who owns the note has a claim on the property, just as the bank would if they were to own the note.

Unlike in an eviction, when a property with equity defaults, the note owner can recover missed payments, late fees, attorney fees, and corporate advances in the future.

With note investing, you can find nearly all the forms of profitability that property ownership offers.

Purchasing notes are not only a unique way to obtain property (especially with vacant first mortgages). You can also flip, rehab, and borrow against notes, or leverage them like real estate.

Whether a note is performing or nonperforming, it can potentially be sold (flipped and/or wholesaled) to an investor in any condition, at any time. Generally, a note is not required to be held for a certain amount of time before you can sell it again.

You can recapitalize by selling what is known as *a partial.* This practice refers to selling a partial number of payments to an investor for a designated term at a designated price. This option can be a great way to quickly recover a portion of the initial investment while maintaining ownership of the note. It is beneficial for the partial-note buyer because it requires a smaller amount of money to invest for a shorter period of time.

Like rehabilitating a house, notes can be rehabbed or retouched by reworking the original note. If a borrower were to miss one or more payments because of an unforeseen circumstance, the note owner (or their servicer) can rework the terms of the loan to fit the borrower's new needs. This allows the borrower to stay in the home while the investor maintains a steady stream of cash flow.

Mortgage notes offer an investor the opportunity to collateralize the note. Since the note generates monthly income for the investor, it can be considered a cash-flowing asset. As an asset, you can use this note as collateral for a loan with a private-money investor. This is known as a collateral assignment of note and mortgage.

A motor vehicle is collateral for an auto loan. Likewise, a performing note can be collateral for a private-investor loan. The private-investor loan allows the investor to recapitalize in a tax-free manner. Since this is a loan, the new private money creates an opportunity for a revenue stream that is exponential because you can use the loan to purchase more notes.

With a real estate note, investors buy the whole mortgage amount so they will continue to receive the payments and interest every month for an extended period. If the property owner sells or refinances within five years (as is often the case), the investor enjoys an early payoff.

Because the note is tied to real property, investors have a backup method of recouping their funds. The investor can foreclose on the property and sell it.

With real estate notes, you're working with investors or homeowners, not renters. Real estate notes are much easier to manage than rentals. Landlords must resolve all kinds of problems that note owners never face. You avoid evictions, maintenance, contractors and tenant communication by owning the loan, rather than the property.

The Cons Of Mortgage Notes

There's always a risk that the borrower will default.

As with all credit investments, the danger is that the borrower will stop making payments. In that case, the note owner must go through the hassle of taking possession of the property through foreclosure or suing the borrower.

Note investors can mitigate risks by doing their due diligence on the property's value, the payer's credit rating and payment history, and the details of the loan documents. Investors should also have a plan for what will occur in the case of a default.

A mortgage note investment does not provide the same tax advantages you would receive if you owned the real estate.

Niche #18: Tax Liens

Another great real estate paper play, besides mortgage notes, is tax liens.

A tax lien certificate is a certificate of claim against a property that has a lien placed upon it due to unpaid property taxes. Tax lien certificates are generally sold to investors through an auction process to recapture the owed property taxes.

The tax lien certificates are first position liens on real estate due to the delinquent property taxes.

Once property taxes are one-year delinquent, the county government will offer a tax lien certificate on the property.

Tax lien certificates can pay fantastic fixed rates of returns, depending on which county you're investing.

The price of the tax lien certificate is the amount of one year's back taxes and penalties. It, therefore, can range in price from under $100 to hundreds of thousands of dollars.

Tax lien certificates fall under property tax law. Therefore state law enforces and governs them.

Every year, more than 7.5 million taxpayers fail to pay their property taxes on time, accounting for over $15 billion in lost revenue to local governments.[29]

Local governments (county, city, township, town, parish) receive most operating funds from property taxes. When property taxes go unpaid,

---

[29] https://www.bankrate.com/real-estate/buying-a-home-in-a-tax-lien-sale/

the local government's method to enforce those taxes is to place a tax lien on the property.

There are currently 30 states that sell tax-lien certificates to the private sector.

Here is an example of what the tax lien process looks like:

> The local municipality issues a tax bill to the property owner. Suppose the property owner does not pay that tax bill. In that case, the municipality converts that bill into a lien (which supersedes all creditors and lenders). Since the municipality still needs to collect those funds to provide uninterrupted services to its citizens, the municipality proceeds to sell the liens to investors.

> The municipalities offer these liens at attractive interest rates to attract investors. The rates accrue against the property and are added to the lien. After the liens are sold, the municipality continues to handle the billing and collections of all outstanding liens on behalf of the investors.

> The property owner then has up to 24 months to pay off the lien with all its accrued interest.

Although the overall process is straightforward, it does require a lot of administrative processing. Each lien must be researched, bid for, purchased, recorded with the municipality, monitored, and redeemed.

Therefore, it is essential that you understand the process very well or work with a fund that has extensive experience managing the tax lien life cycle.

Everyone in the process benefits. The municipality wins by providing uninterrupted services to its citizens. The homeowner wins by being afforded an additional 24 months to pay their taxes. The investor gains a substantially above-market return, with exceptionally low risk, over a relatively short duration.

You can invest in tax liens as an active investor and actively buy and manage the tax liens. Alternatively, you can participate as a passive investor by investing with a tax lien servicing professional and tax lien fund manager.

The Pros Of Tax Liens

Purchasing tax lien certificates is one way to get real estate exposure in your portfolio without actually investing in property.

Investors can start to invest in the niche with lower amounts of capital.

The interest rates create very attractive returns that make tax liens an attractive investment. It provides a very stable and predictable cash flow.

Liens are first in line for repayment, even before first mortgages.

Law and the government enforce tax liens. When the property owner does not pay, it triggers procedures enforceable in a court of law.

There is less competition at tax lien auctions and bids than, for example, investors going after attractive single-family properties and multifamily properties.

The Cons Of Tax Liens

Although property tax liens can yield substantial rates of interest, investors need to do their due diligence before buying tax liens.

Lien owners need to know their responsibilities upon receiving the certificates.

Tax liens are not everlasting instruments. Many have an expiration date after a certain period of time has elapsed, after the end of the redemption period. Once the lien expires, the lienholder becomes unable to collect any unpaid balance.

Investors don't have control over the time that the property owner pays taxes and might have to wait for a long period of time until the redemption period has expired to get paid.

If the property goes into foreclosure, the lienholder may discover other liens on the property, making it impossible to obtain the title. The lien buyer also needs to understand the cost of repairs and other unknowns to foreclose on the property. The national foreclosure rate is 4% on properties with tax liens.

There are not advisors and brokers to help you. You are on your own.

Niche #19: Merchant Cash Advance

The merchant cash advance business is very lucrative, so that billionaire investors from Shark Tank fame, Kevin O'Leary and Barbara Cochran, have invested in companies within the space.

A merchant cash advance is an excellent option for businesses to manage cash flow. Businesses receive a lump sum of cash very quickly and do not need impeccable credit. Additionally, there is no set payment amount. They can use the money for whatever they need, not risking their assets and credit rating.

A business can apply for and receive funds from a merchant cash advance company within a few days versus a bank loan, which can take months.

The application process for a merchant cash advance is significantly less burdensome than a bank loan.

Unlike the process for purchase order financing or invoice factoring, a merchant cash advance company will look for sources that show a business's cash flow, like recent bank, sales volume and credit card statements. A bank loan would rely more on credit history and hard collateral.

How a merchant cash advance gets paid back differs significantly from a traditional loan, requiring monthly or scheduled interest or principal payments.

In a merchant cash advance, a predetermined percentage of the company's daily sales is paid back to the merchant cash advance company daily until the purchased amount is fully repaid. The percentage that the merchant cash advance requires to be returned daily is called the holdback percentage.

The interest a business pays is also calculated differently from a traditional loan. Interest rates tend to be higher because of the short-term nature of the advance and the added risk that the company assumes with an advance. Suppose a business is looking for an advance of $10,000.

In that case, the merchant cash advance company may use a factor rate of 1.20x and require a final purchased amount of $12,000 to be repaid. The rate is always presented as a factor rate and not a percentage. In this case, the factor rate would be 1.20x.

Let's look at an example:

> Lekker Hardware is a hardware store located on the banks of Lake Michigan in New Buffalo, Michigan. Watching the news one day, the store's owner, Kruger, learns of a snow storm heading for New Buffalo with estimates of 4 to 5 feet of snow.

> Lekker Hardware is the only hardware store in town, and Kruger anticipates a huge ramp- up in sales next week in preparation for the snow storm. He wants to buy more inventory like shovels, salt, and snow blowers. Unfortunately, Kruger doesn't have enough money in his bank account at the moment to purchase extra inventory from his distributor.

> Rather than turn to a bank for money (which could take months to approve a loan), he reaches out to a merchant cash advance company for an immediate source of funds.

> The merchant cash advance company, Thabu Capital, analyzes some financial information from Lekker Hardware (like recent credit card statements, bank statements, business records, etc.). The company also analyzes Kruger's personal information (number of credit lines, credit score, public records). They determine that they

can advance the $10,000 Kruger needs to purchase inventory from his distributor.

1. Thabu Capital will advance Lekker Hardware's $10,000 request at a factor rate of 1.20x. Therefore, the final purchased amount Lekker Hardware must pay Thabu Capital will be $12,000.
2. Thabu Capital wires the $10,000 to Lekker Hardware's bank account, which Kruger can use immediately to purchase all the inventory he needs from his distributor.
3. Thabu Capital and Kruger agree to a holdback percentage of 30%, meaning that 30% of Lekker Hardware's daily sales will go back to Thabu Capital every day until the entire $12,000 is repaid.

As an investor, when you invest in a merchant cash advance offering, your money goes directly to an originator (in this case, a merchant cash advance company). This company typically advances money to hundreds of businesses at the same time.

The different advances are diversified in cross-collateralized portfolios and categorized based on business type, risk profile, and some of the terms discussed earlier, like factor rate and holdback percentage.

Merchant cash advance offerings are short (typically 3 to 12 months) and have no stock market correlation. It is impacted by the economy.

Investing in merchant cash advances is incredibly lucrative, but it can also be quite a risky endeavor. Thirty percent of new businesses fail during the first two years of opening, fifty percent fail during the first five years, and sixty-six percent fail during the first 10 per the Small Business Administration (SBA).

The solution to the high-risk nature of merchant cash advances is syndication.

Syndication provides investors with the opportunity to invest in small businesses while limiting their risk exposure. Syndication means that multiple investors pool their funds together to give the merchants working capital.

Syndication, thus, distributes the risk of the investment among all of the investors, which decreases each investors' potential loss while allowing them to share in the potential gains. Syndication provides investors with investment opportunities and business owners with the capital they need to expand their enterprises.

The Pros Of Merchant Cash Advance

Merchant cash advances can be very lucrative and have great returns for the short time frame that your cash is illiquid and in the investment.

It is a great way to diversify outside of the stock market.

Merchant cash advance offerings do well in great economies and in economic environments where small businesses are growing.

The Cons Of Merchant Cash Advance

Although it provides great returns and can be highly lucrative, it can also be very risky because of the failure rate of startups and businesses.

Merchant cash advances do not do well in slow and declining economies. It is essential to balance your portfolio with less risky assets and do well in any economy and market.

The business borrowing capital does not have to provide any collateral. There is no insurance for the lender.

Niche #20: Private Lending

As the name implies, private money lending means lending capital to investors and real estate investment funds.

When you cannot get traditional bank financing, you can borrow capital from a private lender. The private lender earns interest and, eventually the recovery and repayment of their principal in return.

You can use the money from a private lender to purchase real estate (for a mortgage or a short- term bridge loan until permanent financing is put into place), rehab or improve commercial or residential real estate (again, often with a bridge loan), start or expand businesses, refinance credit cards or other debt, or fund a host of other projects, from kitchen remodels to weddings.

Private lending allows investors to become the bank.

There are typically the following sources for private lenders. Firstly, family, friends, colleagues, and professional and personal acquaintances. Secondly, accredited investors and thirdly, hard money lenders(institutions/companies).

As an investor, private lending can be a great vehicle to generate predictable monthly cash flow contractually for investors.

You can become a private lender by lending capital to investors directly, or you can participate in this strategy through private lending investment funds.

The Pros Of Private Lending

Private lending offers investors a lot of control and certainty.

Returns are predictable since you can set the terms of the contract as a private lender.

A hard asset, like real estate, backs your loan to the investor. If they do not pay the loan as per agreement, you can take possession of the property.

When a loan is not repaid as per the contract agreement, the investor can restructure the loan and the terms.

Lenders can set the terms of the loans and create a portfolio based on personal financial objectives.

Private lenders can earn a great return on their investment.

Private money loans to real estate investors are usually short-term. Shorter loan periods mean that you can get your investment and interest back in a fraction of the time, which is great at specific parts of the economic cycle.

It is a very scalable business and investment model.

The Cons Of Private Lending

A loan can be defaulted on, and the investor is stuck with a property that is distressed. It's not what the private lender signed up for, but they can still sell the property to get their capital back.

It does not offer the same tax advantages as it would if the investor owned the property.

In a housing crash, the loan could be more than the property's value with the borrower walking away from the property. You are then not only stuck with the property, but the value of the property is worth a lot less than what you had lent on it previously.

Remember, everything that can happen to a bank lending can happen to you. You are the bank! Do your due diligence and know the risks involved.

Niche #21: Stable Coin Cash Flow

You have probably heard of cryptocurrencies and blockchain technologies. And if so, you are probably familiar with Bitcoin and Ethereum.

Cryptocurrencies like Bitcoin allow you to become your own bank and unplug from the global banking system.

Bitcoin is an alternative to devaluing fiat currencies around the world. You can opt out of your countries fiat currency by exchanging, for example, U.S. dollars for Bitcoin. It is a digital medium of exchange built on cryptography technology.

Bitcoin uses blockchain technology which is an open-source ledger downloaded on computers all around the world. It is transparent. The ledger is available to anyone, and anyone can verify transactions.

It is anonymous but not private. Wallet addresses are mined on the blockchain permanently and cannot be changed or modified.

No person or entity controls Bitcoin. There is no central bank. Monetary policy is coded onto the blockchain and managed by miners.

It is transparent. We know that only 21 million coins will ever be created. We know exactly how coins are mined per day until the total supply reaches 21 million. It is deflationary by nature, making it a great inflation hedge and hedge against devaluing currencies. Investors such as Paul Tudor Jones have positioned capital in Bitcoin because of this feature.

Miners compete with each other to solve mathematical equations. Once these equations are solved, the block is mined. The miners that solved the equation is rewarded with Bitcoin and transaction fees. It is called proof of work.

Bitcoin is a decentralized system of money, and the system itself is virtually impossible to hack into. Each transaction is individually validated, verified and recorded into a permanent ledger that ensures absolute security for each transaction.

Bitcoin has utility value since you can move a large amount of capital from your Bitcoin wallet to anyone around the world without the involvement of a bank.

It has a massive adoption rate and network effect. PayPal, Visa, Mastercard, and other payment processors incorporated it because of its utility as a money transferring mechanism.

Ethereum is another crypto currency which has achieved utility value. The Ethereum blockchain is used to build other technologies, such as smart contracts. Many other cryptocurrencies and tokens are built on top of the Ethereum blockchain.

The third type of coin which has achieved utility value, is stable coins.

Coinbase[30] defines a stable coin as a digital currency that is pegged to a "stable" reserve asset like the U.S. dollar or gold. Stable coins are designed to reduce volatility relative to unpegged cryptocurrencies like Bitcoin.

There are four types of stable coins: fiat-backed stable coins, commodity-backed stable coins, crypto-backed stable coins and soon there will also be central bank digital currencies (CBDC).

These will be built on artificial intelligence, not cryptography.

There has been enormous innovation in the crypto space, and a new crypto financial system is being created and developed. This has created

---

[30] https://www.coinbase.com/learn#crypto-basics

the decentralized finance (DEFI) space which is essentially crypto financial services.

Consumers can buy cryptocurrencies and transfer it to their own cryptocurrency wallets. They can lend their cryptocurrencies to other consumers on crypto lending platforms, earning interest by doing so.

This decentralized finance developments have resulted in a massive demand for stable coins, particularly fiat currency-backed stable coins.

There is a big demand for stable coins backed by U.S Dollar assets because consumers do not want to sell their crypto, since it would result in a taxable event, but they need U.S. Dollars to pay for living and expenses.

There is a massive demand from crypto traders for stable coins so that they can trade in and out of cryptocurrencies.

Crypto traders can, for example, buy USDC (a U.S. dollar-backed stable coin), move it onto an exchange, and then trade it for Bitcoin when Bitcoin prices are at their trade's entry target.

U.S. dollar-backed fiat-backed cryptocurrencies are in demand because the U.S. Dollar is still the world's reserve currency. It can protect you in a cryptocurrency bear market. Also, it can help with rebalancing your portfolio without a taxable event.

The stable coin crypto cash flow strategy involves putting capital into a U.S. dollar-backed stable coin, such as USDC, on a centralized lending platform and earning an attractive annual percentage yield on your stable coins paid monthly.

You can also stake stable coins on decentralized lending platforms and earn a higher interest rate, but it involves a level of skill to execute and it involves greater risk than a centralized lending platform.

The higher the interest rate earned and the more exotic the offer, the higher the risk.

I teach how to evaluate and perform due diligence on lending platforms along with seven crypto investing strategies in our program, The Crypto Investing Method™. Join it at www.cashflowninja.com/crypto

Stable coins are treated as property under IRS Notice 2014-21 like Bitcoin. The interest earned by lending your stable coins is taxed like capital gains. You can deduct losses against other capital gains.

In crypto, short-term capital gains taxes are paid on assets held for less than a year. It is taxed at your ordinary income rate. Long-term capital gains are paid on assets held for longer than a year. These can be taxed at 0%, 15%, or 20%, depending on your income.

The Pros Of Stable Coin Cash Flow

You can "unbank" yourself and diversify out of the banking and financial system through stable coins.

Suppose there is a financial collapse or banking collapse. In that case, your capital is out of the global financial and banking system.

Stable Coin lending is a great way to generate a return you will not receive at any bank and keep up with inflation.

Stable coins lending allows you to borrow in U.S. dollars without selling your Bitcoin that could have a significant capital gains tax as a result.

Stable coin lending is a great way to balance your portfolio without selling your Bitcoin and or Ethereum cryptocurrencies.

It provides stability in a very volatile asset class still in its infancy.

The Cons Of Stable Coin Cash Flow

Stable coins can be hacked on lending platforms.

Lending platforms are a third party and provides counter-party risk. Centralized lending platforms could go bankrupt, and you could lose all your stable coins.

These currencies can be risky because they are completely dependent on underlying assets. If the price or value of the underlying asset weakens, it affects the token and all its holders. If the U.S. dollar crashes, the value of the stable coin will crash.

If the price of gold goes down, the stable coin backed by gold will go down in value.

Crypto-pegged stakes can be much riskier. Suppose the crypto market falls sharply and the cryptocurrency falls to a low price. Then, the stable coin backed by such a crypto will also face a sudden collapse, causing losses.

Cryptocurrency is still a new space, and therefore regulation and insurance are behind the technology.

There is no FDIC insurance that insures accounts with values up to $250,000.

Bonus Niches

Bonus Niche #1: Life Settlements

Life settlements are one of the greatest investment vehicles I have seen in portfolio growth strategies.

Institutional investors know the power of life settlement investments. They have utilized the vehicle in their strategy since it allows them to buy their equity when they buy.

Many billionaires, such as Warren Buffet and Bill Gates, like a sure thing. They do not overcomplicate anything. This is why Berkshire Hathaway invests $600 million annually in life settlements. Buffet even owns a private company that sells life settlements. Bill Gates has over $400 million in life settlement investments in his portfolio, to which he adds every year. So, what are life settlement investments?

The Security and Exchange Commission defines a life settlement as follows. "In a 'life settlement' transaction, a life insurance policy owner sells their policy to an investor in exchange for a lump-sum payment. The amount of the payment from the investor to the policy owner is generally less than the death benefit on the policy, but more than its cash surrender value."

Banking and financial institutions, endowments, and life insurance companies utilize life settlement investments because it provides the following:

- A non-correlated asset to markets and economies.
- Exceptional diversification.

- An attractive target yield annualized and net of all fees.
- Each of the underlying assets carries the written guarantee of an American top-rated life insurance company.

Life settlements allow investors to invest in life insurance policies with a contractual payout from a top-rated carrier when the insured person passes away.

At first glance, it almost sounds too good to be true, and most investors will pause and ask, "Is this even legal?"

In a Supreme Court ruling dating back to 1911, Justice Oliver Wendell Holmes Jr. delivered the majority opinion that would lay the groundwork for life settlement investments. The ruling came in the case of Grigsby vs. Russell, establishing life insurance contracts as saleable assets.

R. L. Russell was the executor of John Burchard's estate. Burchard had passed away about a year after an operation. However, to afford the operation, Burchard had sold his life insurance policy to Dr. Grigsby in exchange for the operation plus $100.

When the insurance company paid Dr. Grigsby instead of the estate, Russell filed suit to have the proceeds paid to the estate.

The case went all the way to the Supreme Court, and the court affirmed that Burchard had the legal right to sell his policy and Grigsby had the right to purchase it. The essential issue at the heart of the opinion delivered by Justice Holmes is contained in this brief excerpt:

"Life insurance has become in our days one of the best-recognized forms of investment and self- compelled saving. So far as reasonable safety permits, it is desirable to give to life policies the ordinary characteristics of property … To deny the right to sell except to persons having such an interest is to diminish appreciably the value of the contract in the owner's hands."

Today, life settlement investments are popular both with institutional investors and very elderly or unwell seniors who wished to sell their insurance policies.

Why would someone sell their life insurance policy?

People would sell life insurance policies when their family does not need the protection anymore, or they cannot afford the premiums any longer.

People may prefer to sell their life insurance policy rather than continue to pay the costly premiums with money that they could direct toward health care bills.

When people sell businesses, they may no longer need to have a life insurance policy to protect their partners or investors. Furthermore, suppose the business was paying the premiums on that policy. Then, they may no longer be able to pay for it either.

People might need more money for retirement. An unneeded life insurance policy may be able to be sold for immediate cash, producing some retirement funds for them to take a dream vacation or purchase the perfect house.

People also sell their life insurance when they have a terminal illness. They may use the money to live out the remainder of their lives comfortably. Or, they may need money to be able to afford the medical care as well as their house.

People selling their policies are in a better position than before selling. Investors can achieve great returns in a diversified and uncorrelated asset to the market.

On average, policy owners receive four to seven times more from a life settlement than what they would have received from surrendering it back to the insurance company.

It is an asset class that few investors outside of institutional investors have had access to, but here are a couple of ways to invest in this asset class:

Direct purchases of life insurance policies require a large outlay of cash along with the expertise to buy the right policies.

With direct fractional life settlements, larger policies are divided into smaller portions and sold individually to investors. Each investor owns a portion of the policy, or in many cases, several policies. This may be an appropriate option for an accredited investor who can invest a hundred thousand or more.

In a life settlement private equity fund, the investor is purchasing a portion of a fund comprised of hundreds of policies. The advantage to this is diversification and more predictable returns.

The Pros Of Life Settlements

You can invest like institutional investors and billionaires buying your equity through life settlement investments in an asset secured and backed by permanent life insurance contracts from companies of top-rated American life insurance companies.

You can diversify your portfolio into a non-correlated asset outside of financial markets and the economy. Trade wars, elections, market crashes, and other global, regional, and local events do not impact investment performances of life settlements.

Life settlement transactions are highly regulated. The U.S. Securities and Exchange Commission has been closely watching the life settlement market for years. The federal government has put in place regulations to protect both sellers and buyers.

There has never been more data, which makes underwriting better. When you invest in life settlements, time is the main risk factor. The longer the policyholder or seller lives, the smaller the return. Thankfully, life expectancy underwriters have become much more adept and accurate at estimating life expectancy.

The returns are great in life settlements. The returns from life settlement investments tend to be better than the equity markets and major market indices.

The Cons Of Life Settlements

Life settlements are not available to most investors and are highly regulated. Currently, you can only sell direct or direct fractional policies to accredited investors.

The availability of certain life settlement investments also varies state-to-state. Currently, direct fractional life settlements are not available in most states.

Time is the primary investment risk and is tied to the longevity of policyholders. There is no way of knowing with certainty how long someone will live, especially in a world where the pace of medical innovation and advancement is faster than ever.

Life settlement investments are illiquid, and you must commit funds for the duration of the investment. Money will typically be tied up in a life settlement investment for several years, such as 7, 8, even 10 years. Even with a life settlement fund, it is not like a mutual fund that people can buy and sell at will.

The institution offering and managing the life settlement investment is extremely important. Life settlements must be selected and managed correctly. "Do-it-yourself investors" can often do quite well with something like peer-to-peer lending. However, life settlements are sophisticated investments that require expert selection, management, and oversight.

It is extremely important to look at the life settlement investment providers' track record while doing your research and due diligence. Ask about their processes, such as underwriting.

Bonus Niche #2: Litigation Finance

Litigation finance (also called litigation funding) is where a third party unrelated to the lawsuit provides capital to a plaintiff involved in litigation in return for a portion of any financial recovery from the lawsuit.

Litigation finance unlocks the value of legal claims by providing capital to plaintiffs before their cases are resolved.

This type of financing has existed for more than 20 years and is increasingly becoming a mainstream funding solution that helps equalize access to the legal system.

Fortune 500 companies, major universities, and businesses of all sizes have benefited from commercial litigation funding.

The capital provided by monetizing a legal claim may directly pay for some of the costs of litigation, including attorney fees, expert witness fees, and court expenses.

Litigation finance may be used to fund working capital for companies involved in litigation or even help business owners pay for personal expenses.

There are great returns for investors that provide capital for plaintiffs before their cases are resolved, and investors can invest in syndication funds in this niche.

The Pros Of Litigation Finance

It has enormous upside potential and great returns.

Investors can look at previous similar cases and look at the probability of an outcome for potential litigation.

Approximately 70–80% of cases settle early, 30–20% go to trial.

In a well-structured and diversified investor's portfolio of ten cases, on average, seven will settle. Of the three that proceed to trial, two will win, and one will lose.

The Cons Of Litigation Finance

It could take a long time to get your investment and return on investment. Depending on the complexity of the issues, cases can take up to several years to be decided by the court, reducing returns.

The judgment can be appealed. There is always the possibility that the decision in a case may be overturned by an appellate court, forcing the process to be redone, reducing returns.

The investment is usually provided on a "non-recourse" basis which means that if the case is lost at trial, the third-party investor stands to lose all of their investment.

Bonus Niche #3: Structured Settlements

Structured settlements are negotiated financial or insurance arrangements. A claimant agrees to resolve a personal injury tort claim by receiving part or all of a settlement in the form of periodic payments on an agreed schedule rather than as a lump sum.

In a lawsuit, the plaintiff is normally guaranteed to receive the compensation awarded by the judge. As mentioned, these payments can be made over an extended period. In fact, some of them are lifetime payments, which means the insurance service provider of the defendant takes the risk.

To guarantee these payments, the insurance company finds an investor willing to reinsure the insurance company in exchange for structured annuity payments. This means that the risk is transferred to, or shared with, a third party, which becomes the investor.

Structured settlement arrangements can also be established for lottery ticket winners.

Americans spend $70 billion annually on lottery tickets – and around 1,500 people each year become the lucky individuals who win more than a million dollars.[31]

The lottery winnings can be issued in the form of an annuity. This means that instead of taking a lump sum right away, the winner takes payments. Lottery winners can then choose to sell those payments later, transforming the winnings back into a lump sum.

---

[31] https://www.creditdonkey.com/lottery-winner-statistics.html

The investors provide the lump sum to the lottery winner, and buy the right to the lifetime payments.

Structured settlements can be invested in through syndications.

The Pros Of Structured Settlements

You receive an excellent investment return, paid out on a predetermined schedule, and you can see the timeline of payouts before purchasing these investments

The investment is backed by major insurance companies and possibly the state where it originated.

This investment provides a steady stream of income that enjoys tax benefits.

The Cons Of Structured Settlements

Your investment is not liquid and, for that reason, may not be a good fit for short-term investments.

Payment schedule and amounts cannot be changed.

Most banks will not accept payments as collateral for future loans.

Bonus Niche #4: Fine Artwork

The ultra-wealthy have, throughout centuries, invested in fine art. Art has been a great store of wealth for centuries.

The price of art has risen more than 1,000% in the last 40 years and has shown a consistent rise of 25% or more in recent years.[32] This asset class has investors small and large and investment funds very interested.

Institutional investors and billionaires have historically purchased fine art. However, accredited investors can now purchase fractional shares in blue-chip art and masterpieces like the ultra- wealthy by pooling investors' capital together through crowdfunding and crowdsourcing strategies.

It is a great strategy to diversify your portfolio outside of financial markets. Fine art was called the top-performing asset class of 2018 by the *Wall Street Journal*.[33]

The demand for that piece primarily determines the value of a piece of artwork. Works by coveted artists are more likely to appreciate quickly. Other factors influencing the value of a painting include the historical or cultural significance and the physical condition of the piece.

You can buy art at auctions, galleries, art fairs, and online through platforms.

Investors that enjoy investing in fine art also invest in fine wine, whiskey and collectors automobiles.

---

[32] https://www.moneycrashers.com/art-investment/

[33] https://www.wsj.com/articles/the-best-investments-of-2018-art-wine-and-cars-11546232460

The Pros Of Fine Artwork

It is a physical asset. It is not a business and or investment where people can do bad things that lead to losing your investment. The market will continue to determine the value, not the behavior of others.

If you buy the art outright, you can enjoy the art in your house, and you have control over it.

It appreciates over time. Choose the pieces in your collection wisely or invest in pieces through crowdsourcing and crowdfunding platforms wisely. Down the road, your art is likely to be worth considerably more than what you paid for it.

It does not have the roller coaster fluctuations that financial markets have and can provide great diversification from other investment classes.

The Cons Of Fine Artwork

It's not a liquid investment, and there is no cash flow. It's an appreciation play.

It has a steep learning curve, and the main barrier to entry into the art world is a lack of knowledge.

There is no guarantee that the art will remain valuable and will appreciate. You could buy fake or fraudulent art.

Bonus Niche #5: Equipment Leasing

You are probably familiar with equipment leasing as a means for businesses to fulfill equipment needs and preserve working capital. Have you ever thought of equipment leasing as a potential investment from the other side of the transaction?

Equipment leasing funds allow you to pool your money with other investors through a syndication to assemble a range of capital equipment. This can be leased to businesses, and eventually sold off or depreciated after a particular number of leases.

The equipment may even be sold directly to the lessee as part of a lease-to-own program.

Equipment can range from railcars, ships, and heavy construction equipment, to specialized medical/analytical equipment or major office equipment.

Typically, equipment-leasing funds exist for a set time, often between 5–10 years.

During the offering period, the fund's sponsor issues a prospectus or similar document to attract investors. This document will describe the overall business plan, the general market and type of equipment to be purchased and leased, the experience of the fund sponsor, and risk factors, among other information.

Funds from investors will be diversified into purchases to reduce the risks of an oversaturated or poor market segment resulting in idle equipment.

After the offering period is complete and purchases are made, the operating period of the fund begins. The intent is to receive a steady stream of rental income.

This period lasts for around five years until the liquidation phase begins. The used equipment is sold on the secondary market.

The Pros Of Equipment Leasing

It is a great diversification strategy for investors. If you invest in resorts, you can, for example, establish a separate company that buys the equipment that the resort needs and leases it to your resort.

It's not correlated to equity and debt markets.

If the lessee does not pay the lease as per contract, you can reclaim your equipment and find a new lessee.

It provides great predictable income, and it offers great tax benefits. As an exit strategy, you can sell the equipment.

The Cons Of Equipment Leasing

This investment is illiquid.

Equipment can break and be damaged, which results in reduced returns. When the lease is not paid, you can be stuck with worthless equipment.

Bonus Chapter:

The Best Savings Vehicle for Investors and Business Owners

Where is the best place for business owners and investors to warehouse their savings?

It would be in a vehicle where they could quickly access their capital. They could reinvest this capital in a business to grow it (investing in new technologies, hiring new employees, marketing campaigns). Or they can use the capital to grow their investment portfolio.

So, where do the best players in the capital and wealth game position their capital so they can quickly access it?

Where do banks, Fortune 500 corporations, family offices, and wealthy individuals warehouse their capital to be accessible to deploy back into their businesses or acquire more assets?

Most people would be surprised to know that the great players warehouse their savings in life insurance companies – specifically mutual insurance companies.

Mutual insurance companies are not listed on equity exchanges like stock companies. They manage their companies on behalf of the shareholders, their policy holders of permanent life insurance contracts.

Ask 99% of the population how they purchase insurance. They would say they buy the bare minimum needed to cover mortgages and outstanding debts for the lowest cost.

Ask banks, Fortune 500 companies, family offices, and wealthy individuals how much insurance they buy. They will answer, "As much as the insurance company will sell me."

Why?

Positioning capital in a dividend-paying whole life insurance policy with a mutual insurance company, structured for maximum cash value, is a strategy that has stood the test of time for over 150 years.

Approximately seventy percent or more of the insurance premiums will be available as cash value in the policy in the first year.

The principal of capital available in cash value is guaranteed along with annual growth.

Dividends paid to policyholders are not guaranteed. However, top-rated insurance carriers have paid dividends for over 150 years consecutively. Dividends are currently around 5–6%.

The growth in the policy is tax-free, the dividends are tax-free. Policy owners can also access approximately 90% of their cash value tax-free through a policy loan.

Since it is a loan used to access the capital like a home equity line of credit, the loan is not taxed.

When you access the cash value through a policy loan, you are also not directly taking the loan from your policy's cash value. You are collateralizing your cash value and getting a policy loan from the insurance company secured by your cash value. This means that the principal balance in your policy is not drawn down.

You can have capital growing tax-free. You can enjoy the effects of uninterrupted compound growth in your policy while leveraging it through a policy loan to invest in your business or real estate.

Your capital is working in many places simultaneously, efficiently, and hard!

You can leverage your home equity, business, gold, silver, art, cryptocurrencies, and stock portfolio to use as collateral for lending. You can do the same with your life insurance policy.

You can directly get loans from insurance companies, financial institutions and banks.

If the policy is structured correctly, it can also provide a tax-free income for life when the policyholder decides to start taking income from the policy.

When you, as the business owner and investor, eventually pass away, the policy's death benefit will be paid tax-free to your beneficiaries and or estate.

In family offices, families have combined policies into a family bank which becomes the primary source for financing for the family, their businesses, and their investment portfolio.

Banks buy as much permanent life insurance as they legally can to warehouse their tier 1 capital, which is the bank's allocation for their guaranteed capital. BOLI, as it is often called, is bank- owned life insurance.

Corporations use this life insurance strategy for capital reserves, executive compensation, executive bonus structures, key person strategies and capital recovery strategies. COLI, as it is often called, is corporate-owned life insurance.

Banks and Financial Institutions will lend individuals and families with a net worth of $20 million or more capital to buy these life insurance policies through premium financing life insurance strategies.

A dividend-paying whole life insurance policy structured correctly with a mutual insurance company is a powerful vehicle to position capital after it is generated, before deploying it back into your business or using it to invest in the next syndication.

Liquid capital has to reside somewhere. As a business owner and investor, you need to position it to have full control over it. You can access it quickly and it does many things for you within your overall wealth strategy.

This strategy and the asset class of life insurance is one of the most misunderstood asset classes. It is an area where most people have not received the correct data, information and knowledge.

If you are interested in learning more about this incredible strategy, you can join our program, Your Own Banking System™ at www.yourownbankingsystem.com

<u>Final Thoughts:</u>

My goal with this book is to inspire you. I'm sharing the best cash flow niches I have seen after interviewing over 700 Cashflow Ninjas and researching investments for almost two decades.

I have barely scratched the surface of each of these asset classes and niches.

My goal is to give you a starting point and ignite a desire to grow and learn within you. I hope this book will be a launching pad for your own cash flow investing career.

Remember, knowledge is not power. The correct valuable knowledge applied to create and produce value in the global marketplace is power.

Live Infinitely,

M.C. Laubscher

Founder and Creator, Cashflow Ninja®

Cashflow Ninja® Programs

Cashflow Ninja® and Cashflow Investing Secrets® Podcasts

Learn on demand from over 750 podcasts available at www. cashflowninja.com

The Cashflow Ninja Cashflow Investors Club™

Join our accredited investor community and learn about an investment asset class monthly and get access to the best deals with the best operators in the best niches as they become available.

You can join the program at www.cashflowninja.com/club

Your Own Banking System™

Learn how to create your own banking system to protect and multiply your wealth in any economy and any market.

You can join the program at www.yourownbankingsystem.com

Your Own Family Office™

Learn how to create your own family office to live and build your family legacy today. You can join the program at www.cashflowninja.com/ familyoffice

The Crypto Investing Method™

Learn our best thinking and ideas about crypto currencies and blockchain investing and 7 of our best crypto investing strategies.

You can join the program at www.cashflowninja.com/crypto

The Cashflow Creator Formula™

Learn how to start and grow a 4th Industrial Revolution business. Learn how to take an existing business online and learn how to build a platform to communicate your message and brand to the world 24 hours a day, 7 days a week, 365 days a year.

You can join the program at www.cashflowninja.com/creator

The Cashflow Core Builder™

Create an investment strategy to not only survive but thrive during the 4th Industrial Revolution, and The Great Reset. Learn how to protect your capital and cash flow and position yourself to be on the right side of the greatest wealth transfer in human history.

You can join the program at www.casflowninja.com/core

The Cashflow Multiplier™

Work one-on-one with one of our cash flow coaches to collapse time in your wealth strategy and create an investment strategy to get you to your goals faster.

You can join the program at www.cashflowninja.com/multiplier

The Cashflow Quantum Experience™

Join our exclusive mastermind community limited to 100 people per year. Our mastermind members meet in person four times per year for a weekend at a resort property to grow their relationship capital. The program includes four in person workshops with other Cashflow Ninjas.

You can join the program at www.cashflowninja.com/quantum

About The Author:

M.C. Laubscher is a husband, dad, entrepreneur, investor, and educator.

As an educator, M.C.'s passion is to share how investors and business owners can create, recover, warehouse and multiply cashflow through advanced cashflow strategies.

Having figured out how to escape the rat race and replace his income through cashflow investing, he shares how you can do the same through cashflow investing strategies..

M.C. is the founder of Cashflow Ninja® and the creator and host of the top-rated business and investing podcasts, Cashflow Ninja® & Cashflow Investing Secrets™.

The podcast, Cashflow Ninja®, has been downloaded millions of times in over 180 countries and bas been featured as one of the top 48 podcasts for entrepreneurs by *Entrepreneur Magazine* and is regularly featured as one of the top 100 podcasts by Apple Podcasts.

M.C. is also the President and Chief Executive Officer at Producers Wealth®, a wealth firm that assists investors, and business owners to implement advanced cashflow strategies, and M.C. is the principal at Producers Capital Partners™, an investment firm that helps investors to invest in alternative cashflow investments.

About The Cashflow Ninja®

The Cashflow Ninja® is a media-based training and education company that is changing the way people learn and think about money, savings, investing, and the idea of retirement.

Our mission is to help people achieve self-reliance, independence, and freedom through actionable education.

The Cashflow Ninja® empowers people through digital media platforms to replace their income and escape the rat race through cash flow investing.

Cashflow Investing enables people to achieve freedom of money, time, relationships, and purpose, which allows them to live their legacy, and maximize their impact for their families, communities, and the world TODAY.

www.ingramcontent.com/pod-product-compliance
Lightning Source LLC
Chambersburg PA
CBHW061254220326
41599CB00028B/5648